THE Fire OF Your Life

Also by Maggie Ross

The Fountain and the Furnace:
The Way of Tears and Fire

Pillars of Flame:
Power, Priesthood, and Spiritual Maturity

Seasons of Death and Life:
A Wilderness Memoir

THE Fire OF Your Life

Maggie Ross

SEABURY BOOKS
an imprint of
Church Publishing Incorporated, New York

All psalms are taken from the 1979 Book of Common Prayer.

Unless otherwise indicated, biblical quotations are taken from The Bible (Revised Standard Version).

The Publisher gratefully acknowledges *The Living Church* for permission to reprint "The Answer to Nicodemus," "Visions and Vision," "Intercession," and "All Hallows Eve."

Excerpts from the poems of Rainer Maria Rilke, translated by J. B. Leishman, are reprinted by permission of The Hogwarth Press, London. The excerpt from *The Cocktail Party* by T. S. Eliot, renewed 1978 by Esme Valerie Eliot, is reprinted by permission of Harcourt Brace Jovanovich, Inc., New York and Faber and Faber, London. Material from *Descent into Hell* by Charles Williams is reprinted by permission of Wm. B. Eerdmans Publishing Co., Grand Rapids and David Higham Associates Ltd., London. Excerpts from The Book of Common Prayer are reprinted by permission of Seabury Press.

A catalog record for this book is available from the Library of Congress.

ISBN: 978-1-59627-051-0

Church Publishing, Incorporated.
445 Fifth Avenue
New York, New York 10016

5 4 3 2 1

To my parents
natural and spiritual
whose manifesting of the love of God
has called me into being

Contents

Introduction   1

DECEMBER
The Answer to Nicodemus   8
Visions and Vision   14

JANUARY
Epiphany Penance   22

FEBRUARY
Fast of Love   26

MARCH
The Face of Love   34

APRIL
The Resurrecting Word   40
St. Mark's Penance   46

MAY
Chastity   52

JUNE
Big Sur Diptych I: Summer Solstice   68
The Red Bull   71
The Psalm-Singers   75

JULY
Holocaust   78

AUGUST
Big Sur Diptych II: Vigil of the Transfiguration   87
Star Fox   88
Lightning in the East   90

CONTENTS

SEPTEMBER
 Intercession   94

OCTOBER
 All Hallows Eve   102

NOVEMBER
 Kontakion   108

DECEMBER
 Solitude   118

Merciful God, who confounds the wisdom of this world
but gives understanding to the simple;
so inflame our hearts with love for you
that we may never be ashamed
to be fools for the sake of Christ.

The Fire of Your Life

Introduction

My life has been an ordinary life, and I am a very ordinary person. By this I mean that I had two parents who raised me in the ordinary way. We had the usual problems any family has, and the usual pleasures as well. I was raised to be a productive member of society as that is commonly understood.

Like everyone else, without exception, I was created to love and adore simply because God is. Perhaps it is the awareness of being created to adore breaking through the ordinariness—rather, perhaps it is the awareness that being created to adore is itself the ordinary into which we all are born—that is at the heart of so much of our disbelief. It simply can't be that ordinary. God's love simply has to express itself in more spectacular ways than the ordinary run of things, the particular expression of each of our ordinary lives by which we adore, by which we live out our yes.

The fire of God, the life of the blessed Trinity, dwells in the heart of all being, of every person, of you and of me. It is the source of the inframutability of energy, matter, Spirit, the convergence of all the goodness of the universe in one eternal moment. It burns away the veil between life and death and enables us to share God's own life with one another and with those who have gone before.

Often our lives seem disconnected fragments. It is this loving fire that fuses the pattern, that is our constancy; it is love that undergirds. If only we will, we can watch, like a child with a kaleidoscope, transfixed by chips of glowing color falling into new geometries.

This fiery love, this burning life, enfolds us within itself, and all lives within itself and itself and all that is within each of us. It is the clear, simple, hidden vision, the engagement that pours forth our life, an engagement that remains on the subliminal border of perception, impossible to conceptualize or discuss, but demanding expression by the cocreative power of its Gaze, concealed from ordinary discursive consciousness. Even as we attempt to communicate this love, we know that only the vision itself and following where it leads will satisfy the hunger it engenders and ever renews by this same satisfaction.

Somewhere deep within us we have made assent for the whole of life, and struggle, rebel, turn aside as we might, there is no longer any other choice. Part of our thanksgiving on each return to its focus and flow is the compelling, elusive beauty of this vision of love that once again has rescued us from our mistaken path and falsely exercised freedom. God has recognized our deepest response, deepest surrender, and gently transmuted all our turning away into this same yielding.

I could write, of course, using the more common language of sorrow and joy, truth and beauty, and embracing death in the hope of resurrection. But so many of these words have lost their meaning through misapprehension that we are obliged to evolve a new understanding of the individual journey each of us in the community of creation makes to the same end, understanding that these words hold layers and nuances of meaning that apply at ever-deepening levels of our lives.

Since everyone without exception begins and ends alone to explore these interpenetrating layers, or, more accurately, to become meaning, there is nothing special about my life as a solitary. It is simply the way I live out my ordinariness, the way, for reasons known only to the divine Wisdom, God has asked me to give my yes.

I have fought against this yes, gone entirely in the opposite direction, done everything I can to deny this summons, but God always irresistibly brings me back. I've developed some flip answers to the question, "Why are you a solitary?" not because I don't take the question seriously, but because there is no possible means to communicate what is at work.

Sometimes I will say, "Because it takes a menace off the streets." There is more truth than not in this reply. Sometimes, "Because it's the only way I can embrace everyone at once." Also truthful, but wholly inadequate. Sometimes, "Because God has so preoccupied me with the

Gaze of Love that no other response is possible." True, but the problem with this reply is that it makes me sound special or singled out. God calls us all to the same degree of union. Perhaps the most honest answer is, "I can't be anything else"; let the questioners understand as they will.

Many writers have tried to unravel what is "said" to society by a life of silence and solitude. This is hard to do without seeing the tapestry of such a life from its reverse, where the threads interlock. So I have tried to turn the weaving over and look at some of the recurring patterns common to everyone, for in the end, for each of us, there is only the Mercy of God, and this Mercy can be the most painful aspect of our lives with which to live, respond, bear. "My yoke is easy and my burden light"—but only to the degree that we are willing to cast off the burden of self-aggrandizement, of our self-consciousness with which we are heavily laden, to be yoked to and balmed by this fiery, purifying Mercy.

Here, too, we discover that the solitary's life is a mirror, reminding us that every human being is a solitary, a unique creation of God, and alone because of that uniqueness; that instead of something to be avoided, this solitude is our fathomless meeting place with God and the wellspring of true relationship, no matter how social and communal our exterior lives may be. Within solitude, we are called into truth and confrontation with Mercy; we are given what it is we have to give in our encounters with other people, who in their own lives are also rooted in solitude and silence, however they might try to shut it out with noise and activity of various sorts as we all do from time to time, even solitaries.

For in this solitude we realize that we are all wanderers, dependent on the love of God to sustain us in a transient world—transient not only because of mortality, but also because we live in a culture of transience and change, change so rapid that it is almost impossible to understand what is being done to us by technology run riot and a course of short-sighted commitments that makes our corporate environmental suicide not only thinkable but probable. If we could discover the life of solitude, which lies at the heart of true relationship and is its source, perhaps we might find an alternative to devouring one another and our planet. True community, true life together, whether in friendship, com mitted love relationships, or formal monastic community, can spring only from a solitude that is embraced.

Let me say, however, that I do not live as a solitary in order to say something with my life; it's truly the only way I can live. The reason for this is my own weakness as much as anything, and one evidence of the power of the Mercy of God is that this very weakness is the source of and potential turning point for transfiguration. Grace builds on nature. I have long since passed too many points of no return to be able to explain why I don't live as I might wish, but rather as I must. My failures as a human being, much less a Christian, much less according to the mystique society projects on solitaries (and solitaries project on themselves and each other), are too many, too deep, and too obvious for me to be other than a sign of contradiction. God in Christ Jesus cancels all my condemnation and makes my darkness light. So it is for each of us.

It is partly because we fear admitting any imperfection or failure that cults have such an attraction. We seem to have an insatiable hunger for mystique, for instant satisfaction of our romantic, wishful thinking, which we project on celebrity cults, suicide and outer-space cults, and the cults that thrive under the mask of any organized religion.

When the cult magnifies the mystique, focuses on the part instead of the whole, misses the mystery, appeals to the desire for dependence, to the shivery *frisson* of excitement that is substituted for the holy or numinous, the whole of life gets sidetracked into hyperreality so that we miss our self, our own mystery, which is found in the ordinariness of everyday experience. Instead, we become caught in hysterical togetherness, the desire for repeated shared and stereotyped emotional experience on which cults are built, and to which the solitary life is a counterpole.

All the words about solitude can point to only one end: the journey each must make, alone, to the meeting place from which God sends us out filled with the Spirit, the Word who will not return empty. There is no set way in which this is done, not even among solitaries (or maybe especially not among solitaries), any more than there are two people alike. It is a matter not of doing, but of acknowledging the deepest truths of being. Solitude is the matrix of self-forgetfulness, not the rampant self-conscious individualism that our culture mistakes for authenticity, and which leads only to ideology and tyranny.

Although there are the words that make up this book, and the ideas that flow under the words, they are but faint echoes of a single Word spoken to me by those who have loved and taught me, by creation, by circumstance, by the silence of still-prayer, which lives in each of us. This Word seeks to express itself in human speech, however feeble, to reassure us that the more deeply we enter into the solitude where Mercy indwells us, the more we come to know Humility, who entered our mortality. There is no use talking of "progress"; one of the earliest lessons is to give up all geometry, all standards by which we measure ourselves. This is the insecurity into which we must enter: not to know, but to keep going.

Writers are often the last to know what they have written. This seems particularly true of poets, theologians, and essayists. The essays that make up this book are more verb than noun, movement than explication, thrust than analysis. Where meanings are plural, all are meant, because it is always hoped that the Word behind the words will create salvific spaciousness, the broadest perspective within each definition or description, to attempt the most precise meaning by attempting to push into the limitless.

Here, then, are fragments. Make of them what you will. If there is light for you, seek the Word of whom they are but poor reflections, splinters of a shattered mirror embedded in the flesh of a human heart that beats only because it is charged with divine Mercy and joy.

Advent, 1990

December

The Answer to Nicodemus

In the beauty of holiness have I begotten you, like dew
from the womb of the morning.

Fill our hearts with the quiet silence of that night
on which your almighty Word leapt down out of your
royal throne, and came to visit us in great humility.

December is the season of Advent, the time of expectancy, of hushed
hearts and quiet waiting. And though many Christians don't make too
much of her, it is the season of Mary.

For she is expectant, and when a woman approaches her term there
is about her a peculiar quality of quiet, a great silence that communi-
cates itself to the most casual passerby. Ordinary noises in the land-
scapes through which she travels become stilled. She moves slowly,
carefully, waiting for the first pangs of labor or the breaking of waters
that presage a new birth.

I felt this stillness most powerfully when I was ten years old, and
my family was living in Washington, D.C. My mother, who was then
forty years old, was about to give birth. It was as if the whole world were
on tiptoe. And then one hot, humid June day, she went to the hospital,
and I was left at home with a sitter. My older sister had been shipped
off to summer camp. And I was very much alone.

The house, which was spacious and comfortable, seemed to expand,
as if the walls were illusion and would recede if I approached them. The
silence grew tremendous as I waited for the return of my mother and the
new brother or sister. Secretly I hoped the baby would be a boy, because

8

my father, in his good-natured chauvinism, had promised me an electric train if it were. I never got that electric train, but it didn't matter because I was given something much more precious.

This birth came late in my mother's child-bearing life, and in 1951 there were no obstetricians specializing in pregnancies at the eleventh hour. As a result, or perhaps inevitably, my mother came home quite exhausted. In the perspective of childhood, or the distortion of memory, it seems to me that I was given my little sister to care for while our mother recovered. I'm sure I had much less responsibility than I recall, but the deep bond formed with my sister during the first few months of her life remains to this day.

Her first years are the closest I've come to motherhood, unless you count the numerous stray teenagers who used to pass through my life, or deliveries of puppies, pigs, and foals I've midwifed, helping these surrogate progeny to develop a useful independence.

The reason for detailing these commonplaces is that over the centuries Mary has been so exalted in some quarters that she has become almost inaccessible to people like me who were not raised in an Anglican, Roman Catholic, or Eastern Orthodox home. She has been so surrounded by nonsense, so encrusted with cult, apologized for with such atrocious theology, that the Second Vatican Council sought a corrective in its sensible decree.

For if Jesus is God participating and revealed in human life, his mother must be a very earthy woman in the best sense of earthy and the most complete sense of woman, not some remote, impossibly slender creature, palely simpering in plaster. For Jesus to be real, we need a Madonna like one of the Low Countries' madonnas, with a peasant's face and a peasant's simplicity, who is not embarrassed to pull down her blouse and suckle her child when he cries.

It is only from this base that I can begin to understand Mary as the exaltation of ordinariness, the quietly hidden Queen of Heaven, Queen of Saints, Mystical Rose, and all the other titles by which she is known. She is a mirroring of her self-emptying son; she chooses her abasement for Love's sake, with no guarantees of any reward but sorrow. It is only from this base that I can accept the apparition of Our Lady of

Guadalupe to Juan Diego. God uses the tools at hand and works through uniqueness in culture, history, personality.

But to have come even this far in understanding the place of Mary in Christianity and in my life has taken a long, long time.

Religion was rarely discussed when I was a child. My father abandoned his Ozark Baptist upbringing, and my maternal grandmother was deep into Christian Science. And though, according to the blindness of that time, there was never any overt religious bigotry in our family when I was growing up, it was understood that while our Roman Catholic friends were very fine people, they were at the same time possibly somewhat weak-minded when it came to matters of religion, especially their outlandish attitude toward the Virgin Mary.

Thus it was that in spite of being drawn to her devotion at an early age, and in spite of the education of years, it is only in the last decade that I've been able to say a Hail Mary without feeling guilty, or use a rosary without being furtive. In coming to terms with Mary I had to start from scratch.

In the last decade there has been an explosion of studies in the long-neglected area of relationships between mothers and daughters, sisters and sisters, and women in general, quite apart from feminism. But unless you have been raised with the idea that Mary is, in a very real way, your mother, your attitude toward her, if you are a woman, tends to be slightly suspicious: Who is this woman and why should I pay attention to her? Why should I ask Mary to pray for me when I can pray to God? How can I possibly identify with her life? And feminism has amplified these questions, presenting Mary as a literal model of ordered subservience, instead of the more profound theological metaphor of salvation through paradox: that true humility *is* divinity, which is the secret, the treasure of the single-hearted.

As time passed, I wrestled with these questions while very cautiously allowing her a tiny corner in my consciousness, occasionally using the beads a friend once gave me, half expecting to be struck by lightning.

Perhaps solitude has taught me more about Mary than anything else. Of all women, the narrative reveals her as most solitary. How could anyone possibly understand what happened to her? By implication she experiences ridicule and disbelief. The very miracle of her life shuts her off from the rest of women except Elizabeth, whose conception of John by divine Mercy was the closest parallel.

It was kind of God to give Mary the comfort of Elizabeth. She had no other.

A more specific insight came one year on the feast of Our Lady of Sorrows. If I'd known the historical origins of this feast it might have been yet another stumbling block, but being happily ignorant and somewhat literal, I celebrated a Lady who certainly had a lot to weep about—and then, like an unexpected wave, the realization washed over me that here was the archetypal Mary, and my relationship to her was in the simple mystery all women share, which is to weep over their men.

I believe this role stems as much from biology as from cultural conditioning. Women are haunted by a sense of loss from earliest childhood. This may rise, according to one theory, from the fact that a woman's reproductive system is itself hidden, and therefore a source of wonder and mystery. It may also be rooted in a sense of deprivation as cultural expectation and cultural devaluation excise option after option, and impose emotional and intellectual blocking.

Learning to live with this inborn sense of loss is a hard lesson for some women. It's significant that it was Luke, a physician likely to have an inkling of this aspect of women, who wrote of Mary that she pondered in her heart the unfathomable events surrounding her son's life. For other women, harder than bearing loss is to escape the encapsulation in which it tends to enclose us; harder yet to realize is that with nothing to lose, everything is possible—if you are willing to pay the price.

For while women may seem more emotional, more prone to tears than men, they hide their deepest hurts—their own and those of their loved ones—in their hearts and never speak of them to anyone. Yet it is this very secrecy that seems often to give women a spiritual toughness and endurance that sustain them when they think they have reached their last reserves of strength.

One day I had my own annunciation. The raked winter sun was streaming through the east window of the hermitage, illuminating

11

various items stuck on the rough sawn wall, including a little icon of our Lady of Guadalupe that a Cistercian monk had given me.

As the angled shaft of light set the icon on fire, my hand reached for a dusty rosary both to protect myself and, unaccountably, to enter the sudden conflagration that until this moment had been tamed by the votive light that burned there day and night. It was then that I realized that the angel was greeting not only her but also me; that the intimacy of bread made God and God made Bread was possible only because of her obedience; that sacrament is the earthly and tangible culmination of her yes and our yes to participate in the fact of the Incarnation.

Annunciations are events of infinite and immense silence, for all that the Gospel records of conversation. The walls or scenery push back, become transparent to reveal all that is, was, will be, and then converge within.

That morning I came to understand that it is by baptism that we say, "Be it unto me according to your Word," to bear that Word by the power of the Holy Spirit, and to bring it to fruition in our lives. It's difficult to describe the impact of sunlight on a piece of printed paper stuck to fiberboard, and the insight may seem obvious, but it shook me to the heart.

I took another step when the story of Nicodemus was read at the Eucharist the morning I was to leave for retreat at a Cistercian abbey. His question, "How shall this be?" awoke the echoing voices of Mary and Zechariah, of Abraham and Sarah's laughter over God's preposterous proposal that he at a hundred years, and she in her nineties, would bear a son.

But the significance of these echoes didn't become apparent until I was complaining to the monks—who are most patient—about my problems with Mary that no matter how hard I tried to understand, most of what had been written about her seemed specious. In response, they pointed to their Cistercian heritage, in which Mary is not only the ideal model for the monk in her single-hearted silence and hiddenness, but also takes the monk within her to be born with Christ.

Suddenly it seemed to make sense, though it is still difficult to articulate. This is the answer to Nicodemus: to bear the Word, to enter the kingdom, we must indeed be born from the Spirit, not for the second time in the womb of our natural mothers, but continually in the love of the Mother of God that brought forth her son, and like her, in the same movement, to bear Christ as well. Mary, then, is my mother in this second birth, just as she is for Nicodemus.

That my heart is still not big enough to encompass this paradox I readily admit. I still feel unease about Mary sometimes; there is still the flickering suspicion that perhaps I, too, am weak-minded. But if nothing else, Mary has taught me to say yes: as Abraham and Sarah said yes, as Elizabeth and Zechariah said yes, as Jesus said yes to the cup that did not pass from him.

And each time that cup is passed to me at the Eucharist, I look into its depths beyond the dark wine shimmering gold and, trembling, I say, "yes."

Visions and Vision

O God, by the leading of a star
you manifested your only Son to the peoples of the earth:
Lead us, who know you now by faith,
to your presence, where we may see your glory face to face.

Flying at thirty-seven thousand feet in a 747 jet is an experience unique to the last quarter of our technological century.

The urge to escape the bond of gravity, however, is as old as humanity, whether soaring above earth or spiritual flight, or rising from somberness to laughter.

The migration of wild geese in spring and autumn gathers the fragments of this desire into a single burning moment. Great flocks wing overhead, waking me in the night, or pulling me from work in the early morning as they begin the day's journey, rising from reed beds, flapping heavily, their voices in crescendo giving power to their wings until they catch the updrafts of the rapidly lightening dawn.

Their cries call to me with longing, homesickness, tugging at my heart with an intensity that increases until I, too, flap my would-be wings, exulting with them, then slowing, sadly stopping, because it is not given for me to join them. But there is always hope.

The view from a 747 is higher than a goose enjoys, and the aircraft is itself very beautiful. The cabin is built on a continuous curve, and the broad wing has a reverse angle two-thirds of the way out that gives it a lovely sweep, leading your eye into infinity.

I was once on a flight, west to east across America, that was an advertising executive's dream. We took off in perfect weather, the engines' rumble calling in its own way to my earthbound yearning to be free, and as the plane rolled down the runway, there was the mounting excitement that, feathers or no, we were going to *fly*, and then intense pleasure as the behemoth gently lifted off and became airborne.

Early snow covered the western mountains and Great Plains, and as we flew past the sun, past morning and noon toward dusk and darkness, clouds began to gather beneath us until, in the evening glow of our foreshortened day, the silver expanse of wing with its two cavernous engine pods led to fantastic shapes rising mauve and rose and gold, and beyond the horizon, visions and dreams beyond speech.

We who by our biology are earthbound tend to study life from the point of view of the microcosm, and from this perspective intuit the macrocosm. But 747s help us to see, for once, our earth as a macrocosm that is itself a microcosm of the universe.

The mystics find the universe, seen and unseen, in hazelnuts, grains of sand, and wildflowers. Their visions communicate to us a vision, a perspective, that widens the lens of our hearts, enabling us to glimpse through theirs a depth of field we had not dreamed existed.

Yet these days, visions have an ambivalent reputation at best. When we hear of someone having a vision, many of us feel skepticism, perhaps provoked to ridicule by a deluded empiricism, a reaction that is more than a little fear of being laughed at for our credulity and hope, compounded by an intuition deep within where the green-eyed serpent, Envy, twists and writhes and enjoys its Eden-born havoc.

This split in us is diabolical. It is one of the poignant dilemmas expressed in the myth of the Fall of Adam and Eve, who were not content with direct perception of God and creation, but wanted something more: the fragmented empirical knowledge that could and would, quite literally, put God to the test. This inheritance from our first parents is redeemed only in part by the vantage point from 747s and other mechanical imitations of wild geese.

But curiosity about visions persists. There have been attempts by psychological empiricists to give us a natural history of visions under controlled conditions, when by definition self-consciousness is lifted only when control is relinquished; by philosophers playing with speculative linguistic patterns that have no connection with ancient documents that clearly point to the root experience of loss of self-consciousness—self-consciousness that is both our glory as human beings and the bane that separates us from God and from each other. These supposed empirical analyses far surpass Adolphe Tanquerey's succinct (and equally flawed) summary of three types of visions in his nineteenth-century book, *The Spiritual Life.* His categories are apparitions, imaginative visions, and intellectual visions.

The empiricists, by contrast, have supplied us with a surfeit of descriptive jargon. They encourage us to dismiss all visions as visualization, self-hypnosis, hallucination, hysteria, neurosis, psychosis, auditory dysfunction, indigestion, or the DTs.

Both approaches present problems. Religious leaders become Manichean and gnostic when they deny the goodness of *all* of creation, when they draw distinctions between natural and supernatural and imply that visions are important in themselves and given in specific ways to the select few. We thus tend to think of visions as occurring only within rigid categories that are impossibly foreign to our age and experience, or, at the other extreme, manifesting themselves in patently silly ways such as Bernini's sentimental fantasy of St. Teresa in ecstasy.

But visions are the stuff of ordinary life, and without them we long ago would have yielded to despair. Because they do not often occur in the modes described by Tanquerey, we tend not only not to recognize them as visions, but also to miss the subtle direction God gives us within the ordinary fabric of our lives, and to ignore the heart's response to the prodigality of Love barely perceived on the flickering littoral of consciousness.

Visions such as Tanquerey describes do still occur sometimes. Someone I know once reported that she had an intense experience of the Passion in all three ways simultaneously while washing the dishes and, characteristically, she went right on washing the dishes through the whole thing. Whether or not she had read Tanquerey, or her director had and she was unconsciously trying to fit that pattern, is impossible to know, but the description, even second hand, was classic.

Our visions are usually more indistinct, more oblique. We tend to think of them, if we think of them at all, in amorphous and secular categories of ideas or ideals. The 747 began as an idea; a united Europe is both an idea and an ideal. World peace might be spoken of as a "vision."

At year's end we are suspended in that unsettling ebb and surge that marks the end of one twelve-month cycle and the beginning of another in the sequence of convenience we call time. The sun has already begun its new round. Humans are a little behind as usual, and while the sun follows its appointed course, we use these days to do a little adding up: of our taxes, our failures, our sins, and our successes, all in the light of projected ideas and ideals we had twelve months ago.

The result of this numerical and spiritual mathematics evokes mixed reactions. Some of us will celebrate; some of us will weep; some of us will go to bed early, knowing that on New Year's Day we will still have with us the horror of starving nations, torture in political prisons, military insanity, the rape of the earth and of our souls. Some of us, having run out of ideals, having denied our visions, will commit suicide.

Paradoxically, when we speak in what appears to be secular language, visions become more acceptable. For example, we might say of someone with new ideas, "She has real vision." Or listen to Celia in T. S. Eliot's play, *The Cocktail Party*, as she tries to describe to Reilly, a guardian angel posing as a psychiatrist, the motivating power of her life:

It's not that I'm afraid of being hurt again:
Nothing again can either hurt or heal.
I have thought at moments that the ecstasy is real
Although those who experience it may have no reality.
For what happened is remembered like a dream
In which one is exalted by intensity of loving
In the spirit, a vibration of delight
Without desire, for desire is fulfilled
In the delight of loving. A state one does not know
When awake. But what, or whom I loved,
Or what in me was loving, I do not know.
And if that is all meaningless, I want to be cured

17

Of craving for something I cannot find
And the shame of never finding it.
You see, I think I really had a vision of something
Though I don't know what it is. I don't want to forget it.
I want to live with it. I could do without everything,
Put up with anything, if I might cherish it . . .

While it may not be given to us, like Celia, to follow our visions to
the end where we are crucified on an anthill, all of us *do* have visions,
each of us according to our individual nature. They are the deep driving
forces in our lives and can be evil as well as holy. Although we may on
occasion have experiences that appear to resemble others' descriptions,
true visions are not seen even with our inward eyes: they lie too deep for
that. To bring ourselves to the stillness where we may come to an
awareness of these visions takes hard work, struggle, an unflinching
examination of self, the kind of perspective that embraces pain and
finds Truth—yes, and even the Passion of Christ—at the kitchen sink.
This awareness cannot be bestowed by chemical short-circuiting of
human physiology, quick-fix techniques, or the casual gourmet pilfering
of another religious culture.

Each of us has an informing vision that we pursue, that determines
our choices and the way we interact with the creation— with our fami-
lies, with strangers, with the earth. It is a vision that changes even as we
seem to approach it, like a mirage in the sands. In the light of this
vision, darkness and foreboding, self-loathing and anxiety become wisps
dissolving in the self-forgetful adoration by which all our wounds are
transfigured.

This vision of God, whether or not we recognize it as such, this
daily vision in ordinary gives us the ability to know, even when we don't
know, the direction of our lives. Like the wild geese and the 747, we
continue on through clouds and night even though it may seem that we
are flying blind.

But within this very blindness lies the perspective, the spacious
landscape, the hope that keeps us from being overcome at year's end,
that keeps us going through wars, gulags, and daily petty cruelties. It is

our hearts' knowledge of our forgiven-ness, the state of being forgiven
that enables us to forgive.

We may be flying blind but we are given sight. Deep within us,
calling us beyond conscious knowledge, is the constant, loving look
upon God that is Christ praying in us, the prayer that increases our conscious desire for that loving Gaze and is the purity of heart through
which we see face to Face.

> What time-besotted earth, lurching among
> the planets, sees God's sense in revolutions?
> Time-turnings in mens' souls are never wrung
> from safety into painless evolutions.
> Not often have tangential lives become
> one spiraled helix. Early on, mistrust
> like some fell Pegasus from Fathers', sons'
> own mingled blood springs. Ashes ground to dust.
> Stunned by hatred, famine, pestilence,
> a night of sense and soul, the old world reels
> toward death: the young impelled to violence,
> the agèd fear. And angels break the seals.
>
> Energy is made of rotting mass
> times measured light. And our forgivenness.

January

Epiphany Penance

‑♂‑

January is a time of storms in the wine country of northern California.
They whirl out of the Gulf of Alaska, sometimes queuing clear across the
Pacific to await their turn to assault the Northwest Coast. They roar into
the continent, one on the heels of another. They dump torrential rain on
the coastal mountains, then surge inland to drench the vines standing
blackly wet and sentinel in vineyards yellow with mustard, empty of all
movement except the pruners, who strip last year's bare canes and pass on.
After pruning, the vines look more dead than alive, an appearance that
belies the explosion of life rising from roots and swelling buds.

Sometimes there is a break between storms. Hot sun stabs between
the monstrous pewter clouds tumbling southward, igniting the hills with
an eye-piercing spring green. Double, even triple rainbows arch across the
Russian River Valley, not those teasing, ephemeral creatures that disap-
pear as you approach; you can walk into them and wash in their color.

One Epiphany shortly after I came to live at a retreat center managed
by the Society of St. Francis, there was such a day, complex with cloud,
light, and water. Before the morning Eucharist, I finished reading Annie
Dillard's Holy the Firm. It left me exalted, barely able to contain myself
as I went to confession and focused through the long liturgy.

That day I also learned that my confessor's wife, Bonnie, had become
unexpectedly and reluctantly pregnant. Accepting this new life was, he
said, a bit like taking in a stray cat who gradually becomes the much-
beloved center of the family.

All of these elements did their work as I rejoiced through the forest
after the Liturgy, thinking about my token penance to reflect and write on

the banality we have made of the Three Kings. By the time I returned, the transformation from a grub glutted with guilt to a butterfly drunk on sunlight was complete.

❧

Loser of Sins!

Bursting with absolution and Annie Dillard I've just tramped back from the woods, feet soaked, pant legs rolled up.

Springs flooding, streams springing from every where. Her soul and yours and mine riot through our solitary meadows crying Holy! being burned, consumed. That's her line and she says it better, but she won't care.

And what about those three old kings? Kings, when the *shekinah* pervades like sin did, and I throw back my head and exult?

One was a worshiper, an incense bearer. Me too. My clothes smell of incense from this morning. So do my hands. Incense, onions, and wet leaves (the onions were in the chicken soup last night).

O but I'm not staid! Not marching solemnly down church aisles or even clutching a camel. Like smoke, like resins on the coals, I pop and explode and riot toward the roof; the cherubs sneeze, the ass brays, Mary laughs at my boisterousness and burning, and the boy-child names my secret name and is burning too, burning all of me that is not him, and he is not consumed.

Do you know about particles? They aren't. Matter is a mutable event, they say. Particles aren't points. They happen. There is nothing but interconnections in a cosmic dance of crazy mathematics and the love of God.

Ah, Father Joseph, you are bewildered, caught—what of these caperings? What of your Vine? I am a whole nation of vines. We explode with budbreak in the spring, whirl, stamp, and sing through summer, and then, with Christ, go down to silence. We are crushed and pressed and poured in the cup Love hands us.

Hey, Father, one of those kings was a priest. The myrrh-bearer. You are a nation of priests. You anoint me for my death and I hear the groan

23

in your soul—you can't fool me—when I touch the garment's hem and you bring me back from the Pit.

Your sins are lost too: I yank them from you, laughing, when for one moment you take from me all that is not Christ and Christ reaches through me. O it's not Official, but I brought a gift to him, too.

And who is that third one, the gold-bearer? Maybe he's my father. Maybe he's your father. Maybe he's all the fathers who were greedy for their children's sakes, or greedy in the guise of their children's sakes. Maybe that king's all the bitter, hollow husks taking him gifts, their power and depression, and their lust, rejoicing in helplessness and nothing.

Days like this I wince at the Fraction and drink from the Cup, knowing each time I look into it I am asked, and each time, trembling, I say yes, sometimes dreading, sometimes exploding, sometimes naughted by stillness in the center. And there we all are: you and Bonnie and the stray cat and me and the seven dwarves (my ma ain't got no respect) and we're all up there transfigured with Moses and Elijah, and can't believe it, and neither can Healdsburg, which is there too.

And you know what?

The beginning and the end we can know seem like, are like, are darkness and nothing, light and nothing—they are both alike, we sing. And in that mutable event is creation, and even getting there local or express, the molten stuff ladles through us, finding holes in our tough webs, and, absolved, pours through the whole Bessemer converter, sparks crackling infinitely everywhere.

February

Fast of Love

Kind Maker of the world, O hear
The fervent prayer, with many a tear
Poured forth by all the penitents
Who keep this holy fast of Lent!

Prayer and fasting, fasting and prayer. The two are inseparably linked in every religion where there is desire for God or entrance into the holy.

Although interest in prayer seems to be increasing, fasting has a bad name. It is unhealthy, destructive, masochistic. Yet Jesus teaches that the two are one, not only by his example of forty days spent in the wilderness wrestling with evil and himself, but also in his instructions to the disciples that they can approach certain problems only through prayer and fasting.

There is no question that eating disorders are a terrible reality for some people, or that fasting as a discipline, the intent and meaning of fasting, have been distorted, abused, and caricatured, so that many of us experience each Lent as a mild attack of conscience and the "give ups," rather like having an annual case of flu. This dis-ease is often accompanied by lugubrious interior sighs, which soon deteriorate into ennui, and finally expire in complete indifference.

While the potential to misuse fasting is real at both a physical and a psychological level, it still can be useful as a means to an end, a response of love to the God who first loved us, an outpouring of this love on creation.

Further, fasting is not confined to restricting intake of food.

Fasting is not a diet any more than solitude is the same as living alone. Each time we say "no" to our selves we fast, whether in a sudden surge of resolve to stop being seduced by a particularly fashionable sort of immorality or, at the opposite end of the spectrum, to give up a good option to make our selves available for something of even greater value.

In this sense, prayer *is* fasting. When we pray, consciously or unconsciously, we make room for Christ's indwelling and the Spirit's work. In conscious still-prayer we gently exclude every conscious preoccupation: activities, thoughts, distractions. We are saying no to our selves, or rather to the self-conscious illusion we have constructed and called our self, in order to say yes to God, so that Mercy may indwell and transfigure us. By this means we are gaining control of our desires so that in the moment when God kindles us into flame we will be able to lose control, to give up even desire itself, to yield entirely, and not to run in terror in the opposite direction when we realize that, for a moment, we have forgotten ourselves completely.

Thus we can also say that fasting, rightly understood, *is* prayer, the famous "practice of the presence of God," or heartfulness, an opening of our hearts to the full light of God, awareness of God at every moment in our deepest being.

In this way we can understand the phrase from Psalm 51, "a broken and contrite heart" as a heart broken open to Christ's indwelling. This heart has clear knowledge of just who we really are in the light of the unbearable love of God that intensifies our desire for that Love, and makes us yearn to increase our capacity for Love to enflame and pour through us. The pain that often accompanies heartfulness arises from a humiliating awareness of the persistence and specific petty nastiness of sin, which is a lot harder for most of us to face than abstract cosmic evil.

Fasting is a response of love, and any other motivation perverts its meaning and becomes an abuse of the creation God has made to delight in. *Fasting is not self-punishment*, and any idea that we can make up for our wicked choices is futile, as the Psalmist knows only too well: "We can never ransom ourselves, or deliver to God the price of our life; for the ransom of our life is so great, that we should never have enough to pay it."

Who are we to presume to punish what God has forgiven, shown to us by the Cross? The wrath of God is relentless and inescapable Love. Simply put, fasting can remind us of our longing for an unceasing conscious and unconscious focus on this Love, which is our whole life's adoration.

Fasting in its narrower sense of abstaining from food is an art in itself but in no way replaces or obscures this larger perspective. There are people who should not fast: the elderly, the sick. There are people whose metabolisms are brittle enough to make any sort of fasting a bizarre experience—and excursions into exotic, so-called altered states of consciousness are definitely *not* the purpose of Christian fasting. For such people, the inability to fast is itself the fasting, a humble submission to the mystery of God expressed in unique physiology.

For the rest of us, fasting can take many forms: abstaining from certain foods such as meat; postponing the first meal of the day (an old desert practice); reducing the quantity of food; or, for extraordinary reasons, a total abstention from food *for short periods of time*—three or four days. There is no "correct" standard of fasting except the impulse of a loving heart.

It is now widely recognized by even the most austere monastic communities that each person must discover by careful experimentation what is the most profitable way to fast. Often this requires a certain amount of ingenuity and improvisation, and inevitably, in the process of observing our reactions, we discover how absurd are the silly responses and phony excuses we manage to invent.

This discovery is itself a valuable effect of fasting because it keeps us from taking ourselves too seriously, demolishes a secret smugness about our incipient holiness—only God is holy—and gives us a sense of *eutrapelia,* or entering into play with God, as Hugo Rahner has described in *Man at Play.* This attitude does not detract from the gravity of what we do but enables us to do it with a light step and with grace.

How can we discern when to fast? Beyond the times suggested by the church, and even at those seasons, it is a matter of listening to and with our hearts for the movement of Love, which is a divine gift. This can occur as a sudden realization that we have forgotten God, or taken

Love for granted, a reawakening of hunger to seek that Gaze that leads us into fasting, into the wilderness. It can come with an experience of the goodness of creation so intense that we are impelled to go beyond the gift to the Giver.

Or the summons may come in a different way; it can be an awareness of and a desire to make ourselves available for the love of God to pour through us on to those who fast involuntarily, whatever their condition, not only those suffering from famine, but also those who are deprived of the richness of life—prisoners, hostages, invalids. Fasting in this mode becomes incarnated intercessory prayer, a humble sharing of our very being with and for (in both senses of for: on behalf of and instead of) the other. A person undergoing surgery is deprived of the most basic functions of life, including breathing. A friend may desire to pray and fast to support the patient, offering to God a simple openness, to be used in ways infinitely beyond what we can ask or imagine.

But, and this must be stressed, this sort of fasting is a response to an *invitation*, a definite call to undertake such prayer. Even if we are not invited to fast as we might expect or want, the practice of listening with the heart enables us to be attentive to the God whose life we wish to share, enables us to surrender, fast from, our stereotypes of how the universe ought to work and our role in it.

As everything else in life, fasting has its peculiar techniques and pitfalls. Perhaps the best way to approach fasting is not to make an issue of it. Beyond the initial awkwardness that is part of anything new in life and is best handled by patience with ourselves, fasting soon becomes part of the daily rhythm of ordinary life.

Jesus gives specific instruction here: "When you fast do not put on a gloomy look as the hypocrites do: they pull long faces to let men know they are fasting. I tell you solemnly, they have had their reward. But when you fast, put oil on your head and wash your face so that no one will know you are fasting except the Holy One who sees all in secret, and the Holy One who sees all that is done in secret will reward you."

Sometimes, listening to this text, there is an uncomfortable feeling that Jesus is suggesting a kind of reverse hypocrisy, an artificial cheeriness that sets our teeth on edge. But what he is referring to lies deeper than this. It is prayer without ceasing, self-forgetfulness that radiates from a life in which fasting has become part of the ordinary round over a long period of time; when fasting has become autonomic, though not unthinking; a life that is surprised by the joy, wonder, and freedom of self-mastery *as a gift of grace*, not a source of pride, which is the most dangerous and insidious trap in fasting or any other form of asceticism.

Ironically, celebration sometimes bursts into our lives just when we have settled into a fast, or determined that the time has come to curtail normal activity to enable more profound inner quiet. It is something of a divine joke that these moments often seem to come during the seasons of the liturgical year set aside for greater self-discipline. To refuse to rejoice with a glad heart on such occasions, to refuse to feast with our friends through the passages of their lives, to impose a private discipline on others, dampening their joy, is not only inappropriate but entirely self-serving.

Practical techniques for fasting from food have been spelled out in countless books that range in focus from beauty to the occult. In the end, however, each of us must discover the appropriate practice, its methods, and its perils. We have to learn to make adjustments for our own physical and psychospiritual needs. One person may need to strike a nutritional balance over a week, another can go for longer periods of time; much of the "expert" opinion in this area depends entirely on the nutritionist.

But if we probe beneath the encrustation of centuries and allow for hagiography as an art form, the tourist's desire to exaggerate, and the lunatic fringe, we can still learn much about fasting from the sayings of the desert mothers and fathers. Far from encouraging self-abuse, our God-parents in the desert were well aware of the need for self-conservation in their extreme environment. Their basic diet consisted of wholegrain bread, dates, nuts, and vegetables. Food and liquid intake was adjusted until each discovered an optimal balance.

Common sense is the key to fasting. It is folly to fast when under severe stress. It is folly to fast if it makes you dizzy: drink some fruit juice. Don't fast if you have to drive or operate complicated machinery. Each of us has to discover these do's and don'ts by the examination of the obvious, but what is not often obvious is pride, which can prompt us to do foolhardy things.

If fasting becomes an endurance contest or develops into competition with yourself or others, quit. It is much better to face the embarrassment and humiliation of acknowledging wrong motives than to continue. It is always possible to begin again, a little wiser.

On the other hand, there may be tension when beginning to fast, before fasting has become an element in ordinary life. Laughter helps, and simply pursuing mundane tasks. But continuing tension can also be a warning that we are too tired to fast, or that timing or perception of the invitation is awry. Fasting requires us to learn subtle distinctions.

Some people experience a surge of energy on the second or third day of a fast. There seems to be a physiological basis for this, as a great proportion of energy is tied to digestion. Fasting can make us more alert, open our eyes to see God's hand in the world around us in a new way, and become an act of worship, joy, awe, wonder, praise. We must never lose sight of the principal reason for fasting, which is to increase our capacity for awareness of the God who is Love.

Violence has no part in prayer and fasting. Impatience, anger, sudden shifts of any sort are destructive. This applies in the physical realm as well as the psychospiritual. It isn't a good idea to eat a lot the day before a fast: go into it gently. It's a good idea to eliminate caffeine a couple of days ahead: some people get headaches from caffeine withdrawal. Hot baths when fasting make some people jumpy. A fast should end with several small meals, beginning with juice and fruit, not with a celebratory binge. And emotional lability is a sign that the fasting has gone too far.

Sometimes we simply forget the commitment to fast. This is normal and human, and when the time is right, we can simply begin again. It is invaluable—indeed, for many, indispensable—to have help from a God-friend to learn how to fast. The purpose of this guidance is not to tell us how to fast but to curb excessive enthusiasm, dispel illusions,

31

and help discern subtle temptations from real problems that may arise. After fasting has become a regular habit and guidelines are established through self-knowledge, the need for supervision diminishes, although it is always wise to have some carefully chosen person to consult.

Otherwise fasting and prayer, prayer and fasting, are offered in secret. This discipline is one approach to the holy of holies, to claim our inheritance with and in the Christ who dwells in our hearts, crying out in trust to burning Love who is our divine gift.

Out of infinite glory, may God give you the power through the Spirit for your hidden self to grow strong, so that Christ may live in your hearts through faith, and then, planted in love and built in love, you will with all the saints have strength to grasp the breadth and the length, the height and the depth; until, knowing the love of Christ, which is beyond all knowledge, you are filled with the utter fullness of God.

March

The Face of Love

Almighty God, we pray you graciously to behold this your family,
for whom Jesus Christ was content to be betrayed,
and given into the hands of sinners,
and to suffer death upon the cross.

Crucifixes are dangerous. Like other symbols, they can lose their mean-ing through overuse or abuse. Crucifixes confront us, yet we can and often do weasel out of being brought face to Face with their message.

Sometimes crucifixes incite us to justifiable rebellion against a lin-gering Jansenist piety that in its imaginative excess appeals to neurotic guilt. On the other hand, while trying to escape, we may hear a little voice protest, "But it happened so very long ago and far away, and someone else did it."

There are other ways to misuse the crucifix. In times of crisis or imagined crisis, when we are feeling put upon and martyred, isolating ourselves in self-righteous superiority with our carefully controlled, non-specific, free-floating guilt, we may catch ourselves rolling our eyes toward it while heaving deep sighs over our hurt, using the sign of self-less immolation to justify wallowing in self-pity.

Crucifixes are dangerous.

Every Lent I seek a remedy for these ills. My Lenten crucifix is not a cross with a corpus on it but a contemporary photograph, an icon. No matter what my mood, it does not allow for indifference, or for the comfortable isolation of generalized neurotic pseudo-guilt. It does not allow me to sustain the illusion of detachment from the common run of wickedness. It does not permit me to say, "It happened long ago and far away, and somebody else did it." It shatters my secret, smug self-congratulation.

Its pain is so great, and the shock of first viewing so terrible, that it takes you completely out of yourself. Only by steadying against an initial reaction to turn away and look no more are you embraced by the tremendous and unfathomable mystery of the love of God it contains. Like all true icons, it is a source of ever-deepening contemplation.

The year 1971, when this photograph was made, is not so long ago, and Japan, where it was taken, is not so far away—no place is very far away in this age of telecommunications, jet transport, and missile-borne nuclear overkill. No one who uses Japanese products, no one who uses goods manufactured at the expense of the environment and the well-being of our planet, escapes involvement in the horror of the events summarized in this picture.

Minamata is a little seacoast town dependent on local waters for its staple food, fish. The major industry besides fishing is a large chemical plant that supplies basic compounds to Japan's manufacturing complex. In the late 1960s, the people of Minamata began to realize that something was very wrong. The government sent scientists and physicians to investigate the phenomenon known as "Minamata disease." The diagnosis was quite simple, though many were already beyond cure. The fish on which the people of Minamata subsisted were contaminated with mercury, mercury that the nearby chemical plant had for years been flushing into the estuary, where much of the the ocean food chain begins. As with all such substances, the higher up the food chain the mercury traveled, the more concentrated it became.

Mercury poisoning is silent. Its effects are hideous; dying is certain and slow. Usually, by the time it is discovered, the damage is irreversible. It causes retardation, madness, blindness; the bodies of small children become grotesque, their limbs deformed, their nervous systems useless. For many people in Minamata, the simple diagnosis came too late.

Eugene Smith traveled to Minamata in 1971. There he photographed a Japanese mother bathing her helpless, misshapen child.

When the viewer first catches sight of the tortured figure of the little girl, the reaction is physical and spiritual nausea.

"Pietà," your brain registers immediately, and your eyes wish quickly to slip off the edge of the page to something more neutral.

But wait.

Look deeply into this icon.

It is Madonna and Child and Pietà merged into one: infinite love, infinite cherishing, infinite sorrow, infinite pain. It reveals the way God cradles creatures whose lives have been twisted from the effects of evil choices—ours or others'. God bathes us with tears, with the waters of baptism, heals us, shares our agony. With tender patience she cares for her maimed image, helps us, moves us, washes us into transfiguration. This is an icon of God our Mother who sees wholeness in our disfigurement, beauty in our deformity, holiness in our wretchedness.

This blind, contorted girl-child is the Body and figure of Christ, and what we have done to her we have done to our selves, to the creation, and quite literally to Christ. In her brokenness, in our brokenness, is Jesus' brokenness on two pieces of wood: now, not long ago; here, not far away. We cannot look at her and maintain our isolation. The inescapable fact of interrelatedness at every level of creation, which Christ makes his body, means we did it. Maybe with a tape player, maybe with a computer, maybe with a car.

Made in Japan. Or Taiwan, Hong Kong, Manchester, Buffalo, Rio, Bombay.

This little girl's death-in-life was brought about by our shared pathology, the same choices that led to Golgotha: envy, power, possessiveness, greed, irreverence, callousness, an appalling preoccupation with the material on a short-term basis.

We prefer to think of sin in an individualistic way: specific acts I consciously choose to do to others, or propensities I acknowledge in myself, as if they were mine alone and affected others only as I choose. But if we begin to understand that the Body of Christ is the whole creation, as we begin to experience in prayer—whether we wish to or not— that we are united by, through, with, and in Christ with all creation, that within this creation material and spiritual are highly mutable, charged with the love of God, we are pierced by a two-edged sword.

Yes, a quiet ecstasy of the ordinary, a continuous experience of resurrection—but that is not my focus in Holy Week.

Rather, it is that my sin and your sin consists not in isolated small or gross acts committed or omitted by our choices and actions, or in some vague, isolated theoretical attitude, but instead that we, you and I, by virtue of our common humanity, and in the solitude from which true relationship springs, come to realize that we are implicated in every sin.

I am the pimp on 42nd Street, dealing in bodies.

I am the pusher, selling drugs to an addict nodding and drooling in Needle Park.

I am the employee ripping off my corporation.

I am the industrialist pouring poison into the bodies and, by advertising, into the souls of my sisters and brothers.

I am the driver of the military juggernaut, careening wildly out of control.

I struggle impotently to express who I really am.

Often I would confess these sins as I kneel and gabble my "Bless-me-Father-for-I-have-sinned . . . " but it is suffering too deep for speech, and true guilt almost too deep for conscious knowledge.

Yet for all of this the photograph is also an icon of our life in the blessed Trinity. We are this child, this Christ, looking in unseeing, uncomprehending trust toward God our Mother, and her gaze of patient love, the long, loving look between us, is the Holy Spirit.

And it is not so much in the twisted body of the child but in her tender, grieving face, that we see the terrible, awful price of our salvation.

O God, we beg you in your Mercy to behold this your family;
show us your Face, on which is written
the price of your love for us,
that by the broken body of your Beloved we may be healed.

April

The Resurrecting Word

∽

I once knew a Franciscan friar who was fond of saying that after the Eucharist we should genuflect to each other because we are all walking tabernacles. His half-joking perception is true, and not only in the half-hour or so following the Liturgy, for by our baptism we are bearers of the living Word, having passed with Christ through death to life.

But how do we express this truth?

This same friar used to remind me that my tongue is a two-edged sword. My usual retort was that it is not for nothing I have chosen a life of silence—or that it has chosen me. Another of God's little jokes, perhaps. Perhaps the gift of these words may be reparation for the other edge.

The Franciscan who confronted me with my Achilles tongue is in good company. Toward the end of my novitiate in a religious community, on my twenty-fourth birthday, the other novices gave me a card on which was written a quotation from Proverbs: "Death and Life are in the power of the tongue," and on its reverse they had composed a little Birthday Office. The versicle read, "Lord, let her be and keep silent," followed by the responsory, a heartfelt, "Amen, *Amen*, AMEN!" Little did they realize the prophetic nature of their prayer.

In Holy Week we are brought to an awareness of our share in one another's sin, the sin that caused the tragedy at Minamata, the share we have in the lives of pimp and pusher, child abuser, religious con artist, corporate extortioner, and arms broker.

In Eastertide we explore the other side of this coin, the other edge of this two-edged sword, for these edges are hurt and healing, despair and joy, death and life, crucifixion and resurrection. And as we share in one another's sin and guilt too deep to fathom, so, even more, do we share in the resurrection of Christ, and therefore in one another's resurrection. We share in one another's being in ways that can either destroy or restore; we are not only purveyors of sin, we are also bearers of the resurrecting Word. By our words and actions we can tip the balance in either direction. That we may choose which edge of the sword we will use is the perilous freedom Christ gives us as children of God.

Scripture is full of references to this sword. In the Old Testament they seem often to be references to judgment: the angel with the flaming sword guards the entrance to Eden; the angel with the sword confronts Balaam's ass; the angel with the sword prepares to destroy Jerusalem, because David's arrogance does not allow him to be content with the lordship over Israel shared out to him by the Lord God, but insists on the lordliness his vanity can derive from knowing exactly how many people he rules over.

In the New Testament the emphasis changes: the angels by the empty tomb have left their swords in heaven; the One who sits on the throne, in whose mouth is a sharp two-edged sword, says, "Do not be afraid. I am first and last, and I am the living one; for I was dead and now I am alive for ever more, and I hold the keys of Death and Death's domain."

Fear not, for judgment is given from the throne that is the tree of the crucified One.

Christ is the Word come to us, "living and active, sharper than any two-edged sword, piercing to the division of soul and spirit, of joints and marrow, and discerning the thoughts and intentions of the heart." Like the shaft of light in an eye surgeon's laser that repairs detached retinas and is sharper than any scalpel, the divine Word, crucified and risen, penetrates the deepest recesses of our selves, to fuse our fragmentation, to glorify our wounds, to bring us from the death we share into the resurrection we share, to graft the Word in us that we may bear fruitful peace, to be to each other the resurrected Christ, bearers of the resurrecting word.

As in vineyard grafting, we, the rootstock, must be cut to the heart by Christ so that the fruitful bud of the Word may be implanted and our mingled lives be fused, for "No branch can bear fruit by itself, but only if it remains united with me."

One spring, years after that long-ago convent birthday, I discovered that my sisters had given me only half of the quotation from Proverbs. "Death and Life are in the power of the tongue, and those who love it will eat its fruits." Or, in the REB translation, "The tongue has power of life and death; make friends with it and enjoy its fruits."

We must be wounded deeply to enjoy these fruits, to have Christ grafted within us, to be grafted into Christ. And let's not kid ourselves: we are all the walking wounded. We walk around with all our hurts showing, and though we may think we hide our brokenness, it is especially in our life together that we see each other's vulnerability, *vulnera,* wounds, and choose which edge of the sword we will use: the edge of destruction and death, or the edge of healing and life.

Or, even more dreadful, we have the invitation to open ourselves to embrace Christ and one another to allow the resurrecting Word, the shaft of Light and Life that is sharper than any sword, to pour through us, to become incarnated within us; to allow God to pray us for each other. And the way to this openness is through embracing our wounds, loving our wounds, understanding that they may become Christ's glorified wounds, and through our wounds, now sharing in that glory, that we may be agents of transfiguration for the community of creation.

If we can bring ourselves to take this risk, to allow this healing to take place through our own bleeding hurts, through our sharing in one another's passion, it means that we begin to incarnate what the glory of the Cross is all about. The Cross makes us guilt-free, not in a pseudo-psychoanalytic sense of never feeling guilty about anything at all, but in the resurrected sense of knowing the truth of our guilt, the delight of being free from the chains of its denial and repression, and the joy of transmutation into Christ's healing love.

As this resurrecting Word has been given to each of us, so we are enabled to give it to each other. When we forgive each other with this

Word, we forgive wholly. Often when we think we are forgiving, we want to make sure that the other person is left with just enough residual guilt to know how much our precious egos have been hurt. But that is not what the healing radiance of the crucifixion is all about.

Rather, it is about enabling one another to be guilt-free, as Christ's death has enabled us to be guilt-free. In daily life it means taking the risk of the fool: to offer love at the risk of having it rejected; to be willing to share pain at the risk of having our own wounds reopened; to forgive so that the other person becomes guilt-free, at the risk of having to forgive all over again; to place our selves, our lives, in the other's hands in radical trust.

It is trust beyond reason. If there is one hard lesson that Holy Week and Easter teach us, it is that we have to learn to love, hope, forgive, and trust beyond any rational base, not with the unthinking enthusiasm of Margaret Fuller, who gushed to Emerson, "I *accept* the universe!" (to which Carlyle, on hearing this remark, replied, "Gad, she'd better"), but in the most ordinary speech and interaction of our lives. At each moment we can choose death or life for one another; we can risk new pain, but also new life, by offering our very selves for and to each other.

This involves radical listening, a constant attentiveness to the still, small voice of God who speaks within us and through the people around us, if only we will hear. In the introduction to her translation of *The Sayings of the Desert Fathers*, Benedicta Ward describes the process by which a solitary went to an elder for a word.

"The Sayings," she writes, "were more than words of advice or instruction; they were words given . . . as life-giving words that would bring them to salvation. 'Give me a word' is a key phrase in the desert tradition. The 'word' is not an explanation or a consoling suggestion; it is a word that is truly life-giving, if it is not discussed or argued over, but simply received and integrated into life."

The unspoken question that continually underlies the silence of *our* life together as we pass one another in the street, or speak casually in the course of daily work is, "Sister, Brother, do you have a word for me? Give me a word. Give me a word of healing; give me a word of life; give me a word of resurrection." How often, in response, do we speak a resurrecting word? How often a word of condemnation?

Many of us have little self-respect, and therefore little respect for one another. So, to turn the question around, how often do we greet each other as the image and likeness of God, with the reverence and joy that calls forth the Word, that enables the other to be vulnerable and unafraid, and in turn to speak the word of life? For all of us are called to be ammas and abbas, mothers and fathers, for each other, and more: we are called to be Christs for each other. This is the glory and dread of our vocation as Christians, that Christ may become incarnate within each of us, that we may bear the resurrecting Word, the Word of life. And it is the Word of the paradoxical glory of the Cross, of which the resurrection is the celebration.

One of the most powerful experiences I have had of this celebration was during a retreat at a Roman Catholic monastery. Never before had I shared so much laughter, so many tears of pain and joy, in so short a week.

On one of the last days there was a break in which we were given an awareness exercise that involved a cup of tea. We were to do it alone, off by ourselves.

I went outside to a hermitage and, after performing the exercise, stood there, drinking my tea, looking across the valley at the mountains. I was feeling increasingly helpless, and over and over in my mind turned the question, "How can I possibly receive this overwhelming love?"

The next morning we heard the stories of the lawyer who tried to trap Jesus, and the parable of the Good Samaritan. The question we explored was love of God, neighbor, self; and my own effort was to know this love as one seamless love, not three loves, or one love taking a couple of acute-angle turns, as we so often perceive it.

A few hours later at the Eucharist, I received the answer to both questions. The Roman rite retains the prayer, "Lord, I am not worthy to receive you; speak but the word and I shall be healed."

In that moment I understood that each monk in the colloquia, each monk I passed in the corridor, each monk with whom I shared moments of joy and tears was not only, to use the Franciscan's phrase, a walking tabernacle, not only bore the glorified and resurrected Christ, but at the heart of this mystery truly *was* Christ, and in our sharing of wounds, our laughter and sorrow, our silliness and wisdom, the Word was indeed spoken, and we were healed.

From then on, as we encountered one another, these words echoed within me: "Edward (or William, or Gerald, or Andrew . . .), I am not worthy to receive you."

Reader, I am not worthy to receive you; speak but the Word, the resurrecting Word, the Word of life, the Word of love you bear, and we both shall be healed.

St. Mark's Penance

⤫

We live in an age of analysis. We pry and poke into every nook and cranny of creation to see what makes things tick, separate them into their discrete parts, and put them back together in a way that makes life easier for ourselves. The language of this analysis, like all language, is metaphorical.

The trouble is, we tend to take metaphors literally and linearly. In consequence, the more we theorize, invent, and make life easier for ourselves, the more we lose touch with the multidimensional unity beneath the metaphors, the sort of knowledge that comes only with the struggle of hands-on experience. There seems to be a direct relationship between the rise of technology and the decline of wisdom.

Perhaps this is one reason people have been cautious about psychoanalysis, or even therapy, when it has been misunderstood—and misapplied—as a technology of the "soul." In the past, British people seem to have regarded any sort of psychological help as a trap in which self-indulgent and gullible Americans got stuck, while on the other side of the Pond, Americans watched with horrified fascination the procession of lives shipwrecked on stiff upper lips, softened only by cream and coziness.

Both points of view are caricatures, of course: the one arises from addiction to undifferentiated experience, the other from a pretense that minds can be cut off from bodies. Both approaches offer ropes of excuse to hang ourselves with, but wisdom tells us that, in the end, excuses must be let go.

Without confusing the helpful analysis that may free us from pathology with narcissism, without creating new pathology by trying to control everything and everyone within and around us, there comes the moment when we begin to understand and even desire a radical commitment to reparation. This burning desire transcends even the new integration that follows on an effort toward self-knowledge, a commitment that "costs not less than everything." Analysis can touch and open and enable, but only reparation fuses our fragmentation with the vision of God.

There are times when most of us experience the sharply poignant tension between what we perceive as our essential needs and compassion, between the instinct for self-preservation and a desire to lay down our life for our friend. As we grow into God, needs *become* compassion, or, put another way, the exercise of self-forgetful compassion fulfills our needs.

Modern psychology offers many useful tools to help us discover how we got the way we are, how we lie to ourselves, and why we feel the often intense compulsion to create a self-image that helps us live out this lie, a self-image that must be stripped away and forgotten if we are to be found in God. Unfortunately, psychobabble, which is often substituted for therapy, simply intensifies this sort of unhealthy involution, its self-justification, and the theology of excuse.

There are few more effective cures for navel-gazing than confrontation with an honest confessor.

Several years before creeping cultural narcissism became a national epidemic in the United States, I was making an uncomfortable readjustment to the use of the sacrament of reconciliation. The confessor, an incisive and creative person, having listened to my woebegone recital, suggested I needed a remedy more direct than the usual psalm or prayer that is given at the end of the rite for "satisfaction"—a practice that often does little more than satisfy our lust to *do* something to justify our selves in our own eyes, to make our selves feel good again, an anodyne that enables us to go right back to our old ways.

"Meditate," he said that memorable St. Mark's day, "on paper, on the relationship between analysis and reparation."

Although the sentences that follow caricature analysis (whether psychoanalysis or other forms of analysis) and set it in ironic opposition to reparation, the two methods are complementary. Both have a vocational quality to them (especially if you are talking about enabling people to come to terms with their interior solitude). Certain basic distinctions have to be made, consciously or unconsciously, in and about life and its processes before reparation can become viable and practical in Christian life.

This does not mean that full self-disclosure must occur before reparation is possible, or that a fashionable trend (in so-called psychological health) is the same as spiritual health. The invitation to reparation unfolds in silence as we become found in God and self-forgetful, and the devouring projections of self-image are exposed.

It seems necessary to begin to understand what the human condition is and does in terms of our own lives, before we can begin to realize how it is intensified by relationship with creation. Thus reparation builds on analysis but goes far beyond it, offering the whole complex of human pain, suffering, and sin, transfigured by grace in simplicity and joy.

> Analysis is tearing apart so that reconstruction can take place.
> Reparation is taking everything, torn apart, reconstructed,
>   unreconstructed, to heart.
>
> Analysis judges and sorts out.
> Reparation accepts.
>
> Analysis justifies.
> Reparation stands accused.
>
> Analysis teaches you to distinguish healthy guilt from neurotic guilt
>   and often leaves you guilt-free.
> Reparation receives all guilt in the wounds of Christ.
>
> Analysis teaches you to deal with pain and your own problems,
>   to live relatively pain-free and to avoid or handle pain-causing
>   situations.

Reparation opens you to receive others' pain as given, humbly praying to be allowed to share in the mystery of pain, to bear it for and instead of, and by this willing embrace, to enable its transfiguration.

Analysis disperses pain by talking about it.
Reparation receives pain by listening, bearing it in silence, and offering it in the love of Christ.

Analysis teaches you how to choose people who will be beneficial to you.
Reparation teaches you to kiss lepers.

Analysis teaches you the ruthless pursuit of goodness.
Reparation teaches you above all to love, to open yourself so that love can pour through you, and that nothing else matters.

Analysis tells you that by shaping yourself up you will shape up everyone around you.
Reparation shows you that by opening yourself to healing in God, healing is poured out on creation.

Analysis teaches you to solve problems by reasoning, verbalizing, and manipulating, through focusing on your feelings.
Reparation teaches you to bear and offer problems in prayer and fasting, beyond words, action, or reason, in thanksgiving.

Analysis gives you armor against your enemies.
Reparation makes you inviolably vulnerable.

Analysis discovers sources of illusory self-image.
Reparation finds true being in Christ.

Analysis teaches you that you are Somebody Special.
Reparation teaches you that you are nobody and nothing.

Analysis gives you tools for living in the world.
Reparation takes the consequences.

Analysis teaches you to display yourself.
Reparation teaches you to hide yourself.

Analysis helps you find explanations.
Reparation offers none.

Analysis teaches you to trust your instincts.
Reparation teaches you to trust everyone.

Analysis makes you self-sufficient.
Reparation makes you dependent on God alone.

Analysis teaches you to be successful.
Reparation teaches you to be destitute.

Analysis releases creativity.
Reparation releases forgiveness.

Analysis helps you find yourself.
Reparation helps you lose yourself.

Analysis gives you permission.
Reparation sets you free.

Analysis teaches you your limits.
Reparation teaches you there are no limits.

Analysis teaches self-assertion.
Reparation teaches self-denial.

Analysis teaches you to grasp.
Reparation teaches you to let go.

Analysis defines.
Reparation adores.

Analysis teaches you to live so you can die.
Reparation teaches you to die so you can live.

May

Chastity

Almighty God, to you all hearts are open
all desires known, and from you no secrets are hid;
cleanse the thoughts of our hearts
by the inspiration of your Holy Spirit
that we may perfectly love you
and worthily magnify your holy Name.

When I made my solemn vows, the third of the four questions the bishop asked was, "Are you willing to remain celibate and unmarried for the sake of the kingdom of God, and, after the example of Christ, to grow in chastity, that is purity of heart?" The wording of this question has been the source of a lot of ribald humor. It's symbolic of the latter part of the twentieth century to have to be asked if you are willing to remain celibate as well as unmarried for the sake of the kingdom of heaven.

But chastity is no joke. Human sexuality, however it is expressed, is vacuous and destructive unless it springs from and is focused by chastity, which means single-hearted living in the love of God.

So much nonsense has been written about chastity that it is almost impossible to give the word new life. To attempt to refute older arguments is futile because their assumptions and categories are dualistic, and it is dualism that has made so much of Christian teaching on sexuality, much less chastity, degrading.

Simply put, chastity is adoration.

In its most primitive form, chastity has meant for the person in a committed relationship to remain monogamous, and for the celibate to refrain from sexual activity. On this crude level, chastity is the *one* vow we can know for sure if we've kept or broken.

If these rather tiresome strictures were all there were to chastity, then it would be empty and joyless. But chastity is much more. It is the agent of joy and the balm of healing for our divided hearts. It is the means by which we learn to embrace all of life wholeheartedly, in exaltation and suffering; to go out from our selves to meet God and our lives in the divine embrace as Christ has taught us, with arms outstretched.

Our sexuality gives life to all we are and do. It needs to be focused and integrated by aspiration, and it is the integration that follows on adherence to a self-forgetful vision that is rightly called chastity. Attempts to deny, compartmentalize, or cut off sexuality by restraint are mere repression.

Chastity enables God to preoccupy us so that we are in deeper union with the prayer of Christ that indwells us, and gives us a unifying vision for our daily lives. We delude ourselves that we pray: only Christ prays. The act we call prayer is yielding to the Spirit of Christ springing from the molten core of Love within us that focuses all our being, and this prayer becomes pervasive in our lives as we begin to learn single-heartedness.

Brother David Steindl-Rast says that anything we do with a whole heart is prayer. By way of example, he recommends that if you come home from a long day too tired to say an Office, to pray a shower. Also to be prayed are gardens, walks, thunderstorms, conversations with cats and other creatures—any awareness or action that engages the core of stillness in which our hearts find wholeness.

Wholeheartedness (or heartfulness) includes the Buddhist concept of mindfulness but has a fiery core. It means not only that when you wash the dishes you wash the dishes, but also that when you are with someone, hearts and minds become united, focused in the communion of one being with another. It means that when you make love you make love with your whole being, spontaneously giving with tenderness, laughter, and passion, not with your mind divorced by sanctimonious piety from your body, which is going through the motions.

Prudery is not purity.

We need to stop asking the questions "Is this prayer?" and "Am I praying?" with all their dualistic and legalistic assumptions, and ask instead, "How is this moment *not* prayer?" Or better yet, not need to ask at all. We need to open all our life to the mystery of Christ's prayer that *is* our life, and when we see obvious ways in which life is not Christ's prayer, to move immediately to the compunction of tears and laughter mingled "like honey in the comb."

For centuries, religious leaders have encouraged overt and subtle hatred of the body, twisting the meaning of chastity into repression. It's no wonder there has been a so-called sexual revolution. But now a curious thing is happening: the momentum is beginning to reverse itself.

The new movement toward celibacy preceded the fear of AIDS by a decade and is especially prevalent among single professionals. Like all such movements, its members have a variety of motives. This movement has the potential both to restore human regard for Eros at every level of life and at the same time to renew the errors of which we have only just rid ourselves; prissiness, a sin worse than sexual license, may once again rear its simpering head. There is no doubt that if it were ever given to me to choose a partner for a committed relationship, or evaluate monastic candidates, you can be sure I would rather have a tired tart than a smug virgin.

This is not to say that there are not rare people who learn to give wholly while remaining genitally intact all their lives, but they are few and far between. And in the event, holiness and virginity do not attach to genital intactness. Virginity is not a membrane but singleness of heart, and many ancient Christian sources attest to the greater value of this second virginity. Most of us learn of this second virginity and the Mercy of God through sexual relationships, in which we experience giving and pain, fulfillment and loneliness, and the free-fall of death at the moment of consummation. All of which bring us face to face with an inchoate and often inarticulate sense of solitude and hunger for God.

This does not mean that we should necessarily seek sexual experimentation before making commitments. The alarming statistics on teenage pregnancy and suicide, as well as the risk of AIDS, suggest that young people are too often becoming damaged and burned out, living lives devoid of wonder, delight, or hope, pressured by a culture that is promiscuous politically, economically, and militarily, as well as sexually.

On the other hand, it also seems to be a fact of life that most of us are cases of arrested development without sexual experience of some sort, without the deep commitment and deep betrayal, and the deeper forgiveness and capacity for compassion that ideally grow from these haunted relationships where sin and redemption inform the heart of our mortality.

We all make commitments; we all betray them in one way or another; and to live with ourselves we need to learn to forgive and be forgiven, to be reconciled with the other person and with our own actions and paradoxes. It is in the process of suffering through these relationships that we learn what commitment is all about, that we learn the price of loving, hoping, forgiving, and trusting beyond any rational base. The price is a foretaste of death, the risk of emotional loss, the risk of surrender in union with the other, even if the relationship to an individual or a community should eventually come to an end.

It is this gut knowledge and the humility that springs from it that strengthen the vows of commitment to another person or to singleness, and these vows are worth precious little without the purification of this learning to adore through the incomprehensible motivations and events of life, through the crucible of despair. We all get crucified at some point, and we might as well be crucified for our own ideals as for someone else's.

I am not advocating going against the teaching of the churches on sexual promiscuity; I'm merely pointing to the facts of our psychological and spiritual life. As Bishop Paul Moore has said, just as we invariably rebel against our earthly family as part of the process of psychological maturation, so we also rebel against our heavenly family as part of the process of spiritual maturation. Or, put in more contemporary terms, separation, experimentation, and the lessons of ambiguity and paradox are an essential part of becoming the selves God created us to be.

Exploration is an intrinsic part of growing up, of discovering identity, of establishing self and taking responsibility for it; of finding out who we really are so that when it comes time to give we have a self *to* give; so that when we enter a relationship our love is not possessive, trying to put on someone else's self or forcing the other to remake themselves in our image. True loving does not need to obliterate self in the other person's tastes and opinions in unhealthy codependence. Instead, as the poet Rilke reminds us, true loving is the delighted meeting of two solitudes who can afford "the extravagance of walking unembraced."

The moment we learn to live free from submission or rebellion is the moment of self-knowledge. We relinquish defenses; we give up sweet anger and blame, self-hatred and self-righteousness; we let go the pleasure of seeing the mote in the other's eye, while ignoring the oak timber in our own.

With self-knowledge, we begin to live passionately, com-passionate-ly, in the literal sense of that word. We let go judgment to be crucified with the other. We experience the agony of the other in our own heart, because we wholeheartedly embrace the being we share with the other in self-forgetfulness.

Here we come to the essence of vows of commitment, no matter what our state of life: they are extensions of our baptismal vows. Baptismal vows strengthen, guide, and enable us to come to that meeting place where in dread and awe and love we meet our God alone and are shown our selves. These vows enable us to stand firm and be purified by the searing light of God, rather than flee screaming in the opposite direction. These vows are a rite, a sign of a baptism that comes in these moments of meeting. They are effected not by water poured but by tears. The evangelical counsels, wrongly prescribed solely for monastics, are a shorthand for the lifelong process of conversion that effects the baptismal rite and commitment.

Poverty, whether springing from deprivation or surfeit, enables desire for God, awareness of the need for God; opens us to be drawn by simplicity, to discover the ardor that strengthens us, to strip from our lives all that interferes with God's wooing. Obedience, the listening, the constant giving in love of our selves for others, enables us to yield to this ardor, to the summons in our hearts, and focuses the ever more apophatic vision until we seek nothing else.

And chastity: chastity above all, in its fidelity and self-emptying, leads us into adoration, which is all of life lived in self-forgetfulness— and who has not tasted self-forgetfulness, this greatest gift of love that is true fulfillment, without increased hunger, enflamed desire? We need to understand that the joyous self-restraint of chastity is a consequence of passionate and single-hearted aspiration, not the empty, bitter fruit of mere constraint. Chastity leads to the purity of heart that Kierkegaard described, "to will one thing."

Chastity is the physical response to our forgivenness, the pervasive and focused compassion of a God who loves us not only in our weakness but also at our worst, a love that is so painful in its enfolding of us (painful because it is pure and we are not) that we can only respond with the whole of our incarnate being.

Chastity is the orgasm of prayer.*

This koan applies equally to those in committed relationships and to the single person or the monastic. Vows are pointless if the motivation is not love and adoration of the God who is Love, a total focusing of our lives in that love. As we grow in prayer, the need for chastity becomes more evident no matter what our state of life. For some, the journey into God is enabled by a committed relationship with another that includes sexual expression. For others it is enabled by celibacy. One is *not* inherently superior to the other. Either way, God is a consuming fire.

Deep conflicts arise in relationships or communities where people claim to live in chastity and simultaneously engage in physical or other varieties of promiscuity. If the sources of these conflicts are not faced and resolved, they become ever more deeply rooted, creating serious psychological, physical, and spiritual problems. The tragedy is that those most deeply affected may not be the ones engaging in promiscuous behavior, but rather those who take most seriously the betrayal of the vow. You cannot make this vow with your fingers crossed, or with subclauses and exceptions, without damaging yourself and everyone around you.

---

*A Cistercian abbot points out the reversibility of this koan: prayer is the orgasm of chastity.

Perhaps one of the lessons among many to be learned is that the struggle to remain chaste is not the same as the conflict caused by promiscuity. The first is a normal tension of any committed life, of striving and constantly falling short; the second is a fundamental violation of integrity.

Because we have not been taught the discernment and skills that foster chastity, as opposed to judgmental control, we fail to support one another by compassion, education, and wise spiritual counsel. Thus we should not be surprised when fidelity breaks down in times of crisis. It is fidelity to self-forgetful aspiration that nurtures the self-respect that is the nexus of fidelity in relationships and binds the community together.

"For better or worse" applies equally to monastic vows and to committed relationships (would that people had a novitiate for these relationships). These commitments are chaste when they are made without reserve as far as humanly possible, as opposed to the attitude too often expressed: "As soon as the going gets rough I'm bailing out," or "I'll stick around until or unless something better comes along."

Chastity arises from personal integrity, fidelity to self for the sake of community, and above all, fidelity to a deepening vision of God. If commitment to chastity vacillates, it becomes the basic source of conflict within each of us and the community in which we live. If we persevere in becoming the unique person we are meant to be, the time comes when we realize we can no longer do merely what we want but only what we must. We must give up lesser goods for the pearl of great price. For each of us, the process of this coming-to-be will be different; for each the price will be everything.

God weans us from the seduction of the material, from our lust to possess. We discover that possession is not worth the price we pay for attachment: the battle for control, the distraction and interruption, the obsession, the frustration of adoration, of self-forgetfulness. But even as our relationship to created things becomes more purified, they become more beautiful and more beloved in consequence, and we more incarnate in the Incarnate Christ. In this experiential engagement we come to know that love is the union of wills *integrated* with feelings, the union of our truest selves focused in and by the love of God.

Our true individuation comes into being with the deepening, darkly obscure, yet ever more alive perception of our fiery relationship with Mercy. Obscure, yet this perception has more reality than any transient sense of immediate Presence.

Christians have made ludicrous mistakes in attitudes and practical workings-out of chastity, whether in community or committed relationships. We have at times attempted to deny that God created us to live within a fluid sexual continuum that is anything but fixed and final at one extreme or the other. Our hatred of ambiguity and the feminine at times has caused us not only to persecute those who are same-sex oriented, but to bury married women, as well as religious women and men, in asexual purdah. Many of us have adopted elaborate social restrictions or monastic veneer to protect ourselves from the very real risk of going out to meet life—and the precious gift God has given us to delight in— with open arms and an open heart.

Neither committed sexual relationships nor monastic life is an escape from the mystery of sexuality. Marriage is not for those who fear solitude or wish to deny the sexual ambiguity common to us all. Marriage is not for people who hate themselves and want to use marriage as a hiding place. Equally, the choice of the celibate life lived as a single person or in monastic community is not for those who have been brainwashed by a condemning church into feeling they must destroy their sexuality, and by extension their personality, in order to fulfill someone else's fearful and static notion of "perfection"; nor is it "penance" offered to a condemning and tyrannical god. The celibate life is not a legitimation of either pious veneer or exclusive clubs of the like-minded.

There is no refuge for those who fear sexuality: a woman becomes a harpy if she does not embrace those aspects of herself she may be conditioned to despise, and a man is emasculated if he does not embrace and integrate the characteristics that a macho culture, in its pitiable terror, may try to destroy. Sooner or later we all must come to terms with the many-faceted androgynous wonder of our creatureliness in the solitude of the heart, and it is from this solitude, from its tears and its fire, that we learn to forget ourselves, to love, and to give.

As social mores have changed, hatred of ambiguity and women has become more overt. People who have been damaged by these attitudes have in turn taken refuge in denying the goodness of creation in all its many mysterious aspects, the creation God has made to delight in *as it is*, the complex and unfathomable mystery of human sexuality.

Unfortunately, in times of change and controversy the churches seem to allow themselves to be bullied or frightened, finding it expedient to join the persecutors in order to justify a history of repressive, simplistic, and linear theology set over against the reality of the vast and spacious love of God. Persecution of, or discrimination against, any individual or group because of sexual orientation or gender is the psychological effluent of repression.

Sooner or later the churches must receive and bless the world as God created it, instead of concentrating their energies on justifying stereotypes, warped fantasies, and bent perceptions. Sooner, it is devoutly to be hoped, the churches must realize that by condemning people for the way God made them, they are condemning *God*, and that no one should be prevented from a call to serve or from a carefully considered lifelong commitment to another person simply on the basis of gender or orientation. But even if the churches do persist in creating a subculture of the oppressed, they will never be able to destroy the wisdom that the God of the oppressed, rejoicing and indwelling the creation Love has made, blesses *all* people in their vowed commitments, even if the institutions will not.

The commandment we have been given is to love God, neighbor, and self—all of our selves—with Love's single movement. It is the same breath of God pouring life into our neighbor and our selves that fires the life of the blessed Trinity, into which we are sublimely integrated as we embrace this Love and are embraced.

As we become more attuned to the love of God, as we become more mindful of the beauty of creation, as our senses become more acute, we discover each leaf, each creature, each human being to be limned with fire. The holy fires of creation call to the deep fires in our hearts, and on reflection, we may become aware that we have responded with all of our incarnate being.

But we must not fool ourselves. Chastity is difficult. It is difficult to give up the single-minded pillage that passes for "life" in our promiscuous culture. It is difficult to let go of greed long enough to allow grace to transform us, to bless us with the true chastity of single-hearted, self-emptying love. The tension between promiscuity and chastity, and our attitudes toward sexual expression are largely conditioned by the way we respond to life as a whole.

There is no gainsaying that chastity completely opposes a society that promotes economic, political, and military excess at the expense not only of the poor and powerless, but of the biosphere. It is this social and ecological promiscuity that creates despair: the materialism, the lust for power that controls by condemnation, the heedless, exploitive technology. Blinded by pain and hopelessness, oppressed people seek comfort in bodily touching, and the culture that is the matrix of their despair has no right to judge them. Equally, a chastity that mirrors God's inviolable vulnerability opposes the promiscuity of a so-called religious culture that refuses to acknowledge pain or any question that might threaten its complacent theological and self-per-petuating ecclesial system—a closed system that it is not difficult to liken to Hell.

Underlying cultural promiscuity is an attitude that says anything uncomfortable is bad and should be excised from life. In its religious form it regards spirituality as a commodity. It demands joy without pain, union without sacrifice, commitment without suffering. It affects not only people who look askance at celibates but the celibates themselves. It generates a mystique, a self-indulgent double standard that regards monastic chastity as "harder" or more "sick" than the chastity of committed relationships, or no chastity at all. Fostered in this hothouse atmosphere is the notion that it's more neurotic and destructive for a horny monk or sister to endure the suffering of the difficult times of celibate chastity than it is for a horny partner to endure the suffering involved in the chastity of a committed relationship.

In addition, there is a simple lack of factual information about the body: most women approaching their late thirties can be subject to an overwhelming desire to have a baby, however inappropriate. Monastic

women serious about their celibacy are not exempt. This feeling usually has nothing to do with the wish to be a parent, vocation, personal
authenticity, or "being a woman"; it is simply the body signaling a
reminder that the potential to reproduce is fading. This urge is neither
a signal that having a baby is an absolute need, nor that a betrayal is in
process; it is a confrontation with the reality of time. When information like this is not common currency, women feel isolated by what
seems to be a terrible secret. As a result, this ordinary passage can
become an unnecessary personal crisis in which middle-aged women
make drastic changes in their lives that they later regret. The same is
true for that old problem of "falling in love"; simple information about
pheromones can free people who feel emotionally trapped and overwhelmed to discern and to undertake the path of enduring relationships.

It's ironic that in a culture that places high value on the suffering
required to cultivate personal narcissisms such as body-building, the
suffering involved in the self-discipline that leads to maturity is suspect. It is doubly ironic that we monastics often seem to complain
about the least pain or discomfort, when not only have we freely chosen our life, but many of us remain unaware of the costliness of committed relationships, especially those that produce children. This
martyred view of ourselves hardly follows the example of Christ. When
was ever it said that a cross at times wouldn't be lonely, depressing, difficult, and painful? (I can see the Franciscan shaking his head, a twin-
kle in his cadaverous eye, "It's always the wrong cross, Brother, always
the wrong cross.")

Even if we've learned through bitter experience that a surfeit of
food, sex, or power exposes our impotence, that nothing will satisfy the
hollow feeling within us, the hunger that grows even as we are found in
God, there is always the temptation to try for an easy substitute. Again
and again, however, we are confronted with the inescapable fact that to
receive the wisdom of God's self-emptying, we must be willing to live in
ungrasping and unknowing at ever deeper levels. There seems always to
be a temptation to sedate this hunger, even though we may already
have learned only too well that short-term gratification is fleeting and

ultimately fails, leaving us more desolate and unsatisfied than before. Our restlessness intensifies until we rest in God.

In the art of chastity there is a crucial distinction between saying "No, I won't do that" and trying to repress, deny, or psychically cut off (as Origen may have done physically) what God's goodness has given us. One is self-restraint (asceticism) born of love and desire; the other is abuse of the creation. When we try to kill sexuality, our life in God withers and dies. If we are sexually dead, we are spiritually dead.

The tendency toward self-indulgence is in part the human search for a corrective to the constricting, creation-hating, gnostic approach that has prevailed for centuries. It is in part a struggle to understand that true asceticism, the chastity that is part of the commitment of all Christians, monastic or not, can arise only from a theology that affirms and focuses every aspect of our creatureliness.

While physical chastity, like fasting, is best learned and practiced without making an issue out of it, there are nevertheless nights and days when delight expresses itself in physical desire and we simply have to sweat it out, laughing at ourselves, giving thanks that everything is still in good working order. As we grow older in chastity, this desire and delight become less self-centered and reaffirm the intensity with which we are giving back to God the life given us, and its blessing.

It is only from this earthed theology that aspiration, love of God and creation, becomes so intense, draws us so utterly that, if we persevere through the hard times, we are ultimately free to be *only* who we are. This response is the essence of asceticism, and in the end any distraction from this incarnate vision of the apophatic renders God's unblinking Gaze torment. It is in this purifying fire of affirmation of the goodness of *all* that God has made that we rest in Love, not by denial of what is most precious at the heart of our mortality.

Chastity is a way of relating that demands the faithfulness to risk freedom in unknowing, to divest ourselves of everything—even, in the end, of the sacrament of earthly life. It is chastity's freedom that bestows the true fecundity of wisdom and its parenting, to the celibate and the sexually committed alike. The freedom of this purifying fire is Eros in all its forms, incarnated, crucified, yes, and resurrected too—resurrected in the fullest sense of the new creation that reproduces itself *now*.

Those who are faithful are guardians of this fire, and it is only by their fidelity that they nurture and pass on this flame. It is the reality of apostolic succession, the passing on of goodness, the passing on of aspiration, the reproduction of the vision of God, of single-heartedness and resurrection in the next generation, each member of which, in turn, must be persuaded not by words only, but by the example of chastity set ablaze with love. And there is only us to send.

Chastity lies at the central paradox of Christianity: death into life, deserts bursting into bloom, the transfiguration of creation, balanced wholeness. Lying as it does at the center of the bodily person, it is intrinsic to sense of self and therefore communion, communion that in its deepest sense bestows the mandate to disseminate and bear fruit.

Chastity is fertile. It gives birth from the very ashes of its fires. It is bound to creativity, to focused life-energy, to new creation, to bringing forth the kingdom of spacious salvation. Its apophatic fire is the salt and savor of creation, Hidden-Word-Spirit, fiery core that is at once completely unknowable and continually irrupting through creation.

Sometimes at the Eucharist we can glimpse the interplay of forces at work in the living out of chastity. One day I was watching someone celebrate at fairly close range. This person had such total focus and unconscious beauty, such deftness and sureness, tenderness and strength, that the thought entered my prayer, "I wonder if X_____ makes love like that?"

Blasphemy? No. What is Eucharist if not lovemaking in its widest, deepest sense; and, what is lovemaking in its greatest sense if not Eucharist?

Yet chastity transcends even the Eucharist. It is reported of a medieval saint that after receiving Communion one day, she was aware of so much sweetness that it was almost like heaven. Yet she moved beyond this experience and said plainly to Christ, "Do you intend to draw me with these things? I don't want them. I want You. And I want all of You."

But in the end, I return to Rilke, who describes better than most the feelings generated by these complexities:

While life still takes and gives and takes again,
from give and take we keep originating:
creatures so shadowy, changing, fluctuating,
yet in our heart of hearts so very fain

to go through this eternal self-displacing
bravely, erectly, unimpeachably;
from day to night, from night to day set racing—
we through whom the life upsprings incessantly

from our own living, blood from our own veins,
joy from our joyance, grief from our own grieving,
all which we all at once are once more leaving
because our lonely soul already deigns

to go before us. . . .

My darkness, my darkness, I'm standing with you,
and all goes outwardly by;
and I would that in me as in beasts there grew
one voice, one single cry for it all. . . .

If I pile my heart on my brain and my own
longing thereon and my being-alone,
how small it's grown,
since He so far transcends.

. . . for what can these words avail
that come but will not abide,
when the call of a bird in the juniper vale,
cried and again outcried,
has all the world and my heart like this
and the fear of death and Heaven's bliss,
almost to Him, inside. . . .

Let it only, though,
find some abiding place and not be so
lost in that space which they can hardly bear,
those stars of yours: for it is falling there. . . .
You let your own saints' hearts slip quietly away
into the very wretchedest enfolding:
they bloomed there and bore fruit without delay.

You great incomprehensible expender,
as in a single bound you pass me by.
You gleaming stag!
                    . . . go ever lightlier fleeing
through your pursuers . . .
but they, Unreachable, are only seeing
the parted world behind you reunite.

June

Big Sur Diptych I: Summer Solstice

❧

Big Sur is one of the wildest, most spectacular coasts in the world. It runs some eighty miles down the edge of California from Carmel to San Luis Obispo. There are no power lines for much of its length, and telephones are unreliable. In some places, the road is two-lane only by name: sections of it are forever falling into the sea, or buried by landslides from the mountains that rise straight from the ocean floor and overhang it. Some slides take years to clear. These slides cut off the sparse population from north-south communication, and the single east-west paved road over the coastal range can cause vertigo in the most intrepid.

For nearly two years as health and circumstance allowed, I lived in a tent pitched on a south-facing slope twenty-three hundred feet above the sea, through all seasons of Big Sur's Mediterranean climate. There were hurricane-force winds that rolled monstrous waves unimpeded from Japan and smashed them against the cliffs with such force that the earth trembled; there were torrential rains, sleet and frost, and months-long stretches of calm sunshine.

These were months refulgent with stillness and the leisure to be and to observe. I watched lizards catch moths, the seasonal flights of birds, weather forming over the broad bay, the changing angle of the sun in the slow evening as the molten sphere flamed its way down the vault of heaven to slip into a sapphire sea. At night I would be visited by coons and foxes, and sometimes a mountain lion's scream from nearby brush would shatter the dark. The faint roar of surf wafted upward through the silence; the slow, wheeling dance of constellations turned overhead.

It sounds idyllic, and it was. But violating this chastity of wildness were flights of experimental aircraft and things that might not so easily be described as aircraft flying low in the dark, so low I could see the heads of the crews bathed in the red glow of the flight decks. One of these craft, I

68

know now, was a prototype of the B-1 bomber, but I will never forget that night when the strange whoosh of its engines jerked me from sleep, and I gazed in horrified fascination at the bizarre shape skimming the mountain at treetop level. In daylight hours, B-52s patrolled high overhead, and sometimes the shriek of fighter-bombers—planes with tail configurations even a commercial airline captain could not identify—would ricochet off the sea and reverberate against the cliffs.

Looking across the Pacific toward the rim of the world, I would see one or sometimes a small group of specks coming toward me flat out, two feet above the waves. In the moment you thought they would surely slam straight into the rock they would pull up, terrain-following. Only a few hundred feet horizontally from me they would howl past, bristling with missiles, gradually, then sharply, climbing to clear the peak that rose another twenty-five hundred feet, half a mile beyond my perch.

I got to know the regulars among the pilots. We developed a strange, waving acquaintance, an eerie well-wishing between people dedicated to opposite ends and means. They knew I was a nun from my tunic and my location; I knew they carried nuclear weapons.

So we do not lose heart. Though our outer nature is wasting away, our inner nature is being renewed every day. For this slight momentary affliction is preparing for us an eternal weight of glory beyond all comparison, because we look not to the things that are seen but to the things that are unseen; for the things that are seen are transient, but the things that are unseen are eternal.

The Hebrew word for "glory," as in "the glory of God," is *kavod*. It carries the nuance of weight, of density. It conveys a notion of holiness entirely opposite to some Greek ideas. In the West, we commonly think of holiness in Greek terms, as if the holier something is, the more ethereal it becomes.

But the Hebrew word emphasizes the importance of our bodiliness. Like many similar insights, it is also metaphorically consonant with today's physics. Space-time is curved by the mass of concentrated energy-becoming-matter such as our earth, such as a human being. Glory concentrates our being and transfigures what is around us.

The Big Sur Diptychs were written when this idea of holiness-as-density had just broken open my perceptions. It has become an implicit assumption. I had always been suspicious of the Greek melting-into-nothingness anyway: it was only superficially aesthetic; it went contrary to evidence; it denied the holiness of messy, incarnate reality.

I don't understand enough physics to hope to explore the ramifications of *kavod*; but perhaps Red Bull, Psalm-Singers, Star Fox, and the lightnings and fogs of the Vigil will arouse the interest of someone more competent than I to further travel these endless reaches of light.

The Red Bull

-&

Last evening on my way to the tent I saw a coyote leap out of the junk pile at the dump. The hair on my neck stood up; I watched him disappear into the pines, and as I approached he was there again, leaping through the high, dry grass. There was the sense of other life about, and as I rounded the line of trees I met a huge cow, bulging with an unborn calf.

Cows almost wrecked my tent in another place before I got an enclosure fence up; these are strays from the next ranch. There must be a fence down along the creek in the canyon.

Fearful for my fragile shelter, I pick up pieces of earth and start pelting the cow to get her to move off down the mountain, back across the creek. She is strangely unmoved.

Something deep inside gives a warning, and I turn. Not twenty feet away, just below the brow of the hill, an enormous red bull is shaking his horns in disapproval at my mistreatment of his cow. With him are four other cows, more flighty and nervous than the one I have been assaulting.

In spite of my fear, I am transfixed. This is no ordinary domestic bull, lumpish and dull, hopelessly nervous or insane. This is the bull I met on a hike last January, but winter on the mountain has hardened him. He is secure in his power. Who knows what he has encountered in these months? I have seen him climbing vertical slopes, seen him on the way to water at the creek. Has he fought coyotes off from newborn calves, or encountered the cougar hunting an easy meal?

The red of his hide is intensified by the red-gold evening light; there is a sheen to it like kimono silk, like the red-gold embroidery on an obi I once had. His muscles are hard and flat and smooth under the supple, taut skin; his eyes are clear under his straight horns. He is relaxed yet alert; coiled potential. He is vitality, virility, Eros, and Eros transfiguring itself. He is the love of God in creation, the hidden fire revealed in creation.

Here is a bull to dance with, straight horns to grasp and vault over in ecstasy, grasping dread and death, grasping mortality and transfiguring it with mortality. Here is a bull to charge the senses, to communicate the very life-ness of things.

I speak to him, apologizing for my aggression to his cow, and he resumes eating, watching me out of the corner of his eye. I slip down though the pines to my tent, make a few adjustments in case there is a cattle raid to avenge my hostile act, and climb once more through the dark passage in the pines.

He is there: startled this time as I emerge, his head jerks up. I speak to him again, and he relaxes, lowering his head to eat. But he marks every ten feet of my progress past him by raising his head, making sure I will behave myself in his presence. I have broken protocol, not enough to be charged, but enough to be put on warning. I avert my eyes to lessen any possible interpretation of aggression, quietly pass by him and on down to the monastery for the night. I am not brave enough to risk meeting him in the dark on the way to midnight vigils. Behind me he grazes, glowing in the fading light.

All night and next morning I am caught by the bull. I dance with him in my dreams. At dawn I return to my tent, but he is gone and the cows with him, no vengeance taken for my intrusion.

The myths of the Greeks and Cretans come consciously to mind now: Zeus and Europa; the frescoes of red bulls at Knossos; Mary Renault's *The King Must Die*, which I have read again and again. Now I understand: now I understand the bull-calf at Horeb, the yearning for vitality, the sign of potency and life in the desert. Now I understand the making of bull-gods, the suicidal bull-dances of the Mediterranean, and, by extension, the bloody rituals in Spain. Suits of light process through my mind, and black Muria bulls charge into the ring.

Pagan: I am pagan if this is paganism, and thank God. It is part of the genius of Christianity that incorporates primordial religious signs in its vision of the sacred, created signs of incarnation, arrows pointing back to that event two thousand years ago, and arrows pointing forward from the beginning of life. There is a naturalness about the liturgy, the Spirit's activity recapitulating in our own lives the events and mysteries of these special days. This is the pagan sense baptized in the Light; the unity of all things, the immanence of God, utter transcendence.

There are not four loves, nor two; there is only One. And I have seen this single unspeakable movement of Love in the bull, its transmutations, its forms and expressions, its earthedness, and in that very earthedness, the potency of mortality transfigured. As mute, as clumsy, as tongue-tied as such moments leave us, the Word yet seeks expression, even though by moving from direct perception to fumbling concepts, most of what we have been given is lost.

We move inward: this is our movement. Gazing on and united to that hidden Face of fire we are expanded, bursting from bondage into boundlessness, uncontainable, hurled outward by the force, the divine energy, the Fire (God's movement is outward). Even our bodies cannot contain it, this light of union. It shines in the glory of the human face, the glory of God radiating from the glory of the human face.

As we grow in single-heartedness, as the density of our *pointe vierge* increases, as the glory intensifies, we cannot but break out beyond mortality, just as the fruit tree's fire is the sign of its fullness, its fruitfulness. Though its seeds have fallen into the ground, and though its leaves will soon be dust, their fires expand to a spectrum of color so broad, so intense, that it cannot but resolve into white light. There is a link, an inseparable bond between our physiochemistry and our divinity, not a linear dualism but a spatial continuum. What is fully incarnate reveals transfiguration within. Humility is divinity.

It is only at the end of life that we burst into flame, come to wisdom and fruition, only to die, yet this is not a waste or cause for cynicism. We cannot do otherwise. By the fruitfulness of contemplative being Love has expanded us beyond mortality's containment: we cannot but die.

This glory within us arcs across the barriers of death, deep calling to deep, to mingle finally and fully with the glory of the Creator. We are incarnated with one hand, given fire and glory with the other. What do accomplishment or doing, what do material fruits matter in this light? They matter not at all, for matter is fired and transfigured with density of being. It is the fullness of the curvature our being has made that signifies; the fullness with which we have gathered that density, enlarged our capacity for that density by embracing our fate, receiving and glorying in mortality, the godness, the likeness, the image that is caught for a time, its beauty, its terror and dread. The veil is no more.

The red-goldness of fruition links all creation: redness of the bull; leaves on fire—fruit trees and squalid old poison oak become burning bushes; joyousness of birdsong at rosy dawn and russet dusk; ruddiness in aged women and men; red-and-gold silk vestments; the blood of martyrs become bread for us in the fire of Love; fire of the Trinity, dancing wheel of love flaming in our center.

O Trinity of blessed light: your fiery sun goes its way, diffusing red-gold light through mortality, though life-giving atmosphere, to remind us that beyond the darkness is another day. O Unity of humble might, the flame colors of evening speak to us of fruition, the tiredness of time spent, bodies spent, lives spent in your Day. With night weariness presses down while our restless spirits, dreaming, contemplate your mysteries. United to you our sleep is healing of body and spirit. We rest in You, we dance with You, we burn for You. Bring us into the fire of your life. *Amen.*

The Psalm-Singers

-❖-

Sometimes when I bow before the glory of God, singing the doxology at the end of a psalm, I see from the corner of my eye, as mirrors reflect into other mirrors, an infinite line of shimmering figures bowing with me. Sometimes I see them en masse, as crowds are painted in early Byzantine art. Or sometimes I see a lone shepherd or hermit, voice roughened by years of singing against wind and sun, wandering in solitude.

There is a reality to the communion of saints that becomes transparently apparent through psalmody, a reality that has force and power, a there-ness that seems more fully manifest in this way than any other. The music of the long-vanished psalm-singers lingers in the silence. You can feel it in churches; you can feel it in ruins; you can feel it wandering through mountains where holy ones have lived.

It's more than the knowledge of three thousand years of David's musical heirs, more than the psalms themselves, or the shock of recognition that sometimes comes at night when, from a crystalline sky, stars dangle over horizon's edge, and Psalm 8 echoes unceasingly: "When I consider your heavens, the work of your fingers, the moon and the stars you have set in their courses, who are we that you should be mindful of us, your only-begotten that you should seek us out?"

Big Sur is far enough from the lights of civilization that the stars hang one behind another. There is depth in the heavens, a depth that draws you, an expansive infinity, an abyss that opens to eternity, a dark window into the apophatic, pointed with stars, with worlds and universes being born and dying, all rushing toward something at great speed. Yet the One who creates this unimaginable vastness merely with "fingers," is mindful of us, seeks us out, and the awe of seeking ravishes our senses and not-senses, looking into the dark abyss of creating Love.

As we gaze, we realize our union with the divine assembly: at one time or another in their lives, each of the psalm-singers must have looked into these same heavens, humbled by God's seeking. They too bowed before the unfathomable, incomprehensible knowledge that the Maker of the starry abyss pursues us through our mortality, exalts us as sons and daughters especially in our mortality, engages us even as we are formed in the womb, receives our longings, is faithful beyond our ability to ask, imagine, or respond.

Often the psalm-singers seem unreal to us, two-dimensional paper cutouts on a flat plane; the personae of an ephemeral drama that is presented once and fades; figures in a diorama depicting a culture remote in its strangeness. The best biography portrays a fantasy, and hagiography feeds the phantasmagorical.

That these strangers were also psalm-singers adds the fourth dimension. They too were moved to muteness; only psalmody could begin to express the Love at work within, the bewildering darkness, the consuming desire for the radiant Face. They too wept in frustration at sparks momentarily manifest, drawing them deeper into free-falling lostness, manna-filled desert, dew-fallen music, bread of faithfulness, bread of faith.

They sang, sing, through nights and days, heat and cold, in home and hearth, desert and monastery, in dressing-gowns, skins, heavy wool, jeans, ornate great-schemas, leaning in the weariness of the small hours against a bed, a stone wall, a carved misericord or, as I once did at midnight with a Cistercian friend, against the hard, plastic seats of the New York subway.

But now there is no day or night for them as they sing: their time-bound, time-hallowed music lingers with us, though we know there is no time, only motion and bending of space-time. Their density, their holiness, their heart-songs bend with us, bend the continuum, bend before the glory of God, with the glory of God. And as we bow before this glory, we too add density, become mirrored in those mirrors, become massed in those masses, people become Eucharist, one Bread for all.

July

Holocaust

-&

One of the horrors of the Second World War was the extermination of 60 percent of the Jewish population, some six or seven million souls. The Holocaust has unleashed a flood of books written by Jews who survived or escaped the concentration camps, by their children, by their doctors, and by non-Jews as well.

Some years ago, a theology professor wrote to an old student, "I gave a talk on my trip this summer to Poland, Russia, Denmark and Israel with the President's Commission on the Holocaust, along with Elie Wiesel. . . . The impact of Wiesel on me has been very deep, and the issues the Holocaust raises for me theologically have to be confronted. I feel an increasing need to re-establish the Jewish roots of the Christian faith, and to find ways to talk about hope and victory in spite of the Holocaust, which is a pretty stern negation of any facile triumphalism."

About the same time, a different academic friend explored this same troubling topic: "I am about to go off to the College of the Holy Cross in Worcester to give four days of lectures on 'The Christian understanding of the Holocaust.' When you have some extra time, try to work that one out! It is now a problem for Christian theology—how do you work out a theodicy in which God appeared to be absent for a long decade, when the forces of the devil were unleashed—that is, of course, if you can believe that 'forces of the devil' are unleashed."

Well, yes, as a matter of fact I can believe that such forces from time to time are unleashed. I have only to look within myself to see the resonances of some of my choices. And while I've sought in vain for the "extra time" to ponder the Holocaust, there is part of me that struggles with it all the time.

Often, when confronted with unbearable pain and the nightmarish impulses common to humanity, I've taken refuge in Job, who, presented with the incomprehensibility of the works of men and God says, "I have spoken of things which I have not understood, things too wonderful for me to know. I knew of thee then only by report, but now I see with my own eyes. Therefore I melt away, I repent in dust and ashes."

Job's response is not a cop-out, even if it is part of the tacked-on ending to the book. But neither is it adequate. To assume that we have any competence to sort out the interwoven strands of free will, evil, and the redemptive love of God is presumption. Having said this, we must at the same time find ways to face and to think about these tangled questions.

Once when I was studying Hebrew at a local synagogue, the class became sidetracked by a discussion of Hasidic mysticism, which has meant much in my life. Something that day caused me, sitting there in my monastic habit, to wax eloquent, and when I ran out of words, the rabbi asked me in all seriousness why I didn't convert to Judaism.

Stunned, I blurted out the first words that came to my lips: "Because it would be a presumption to deliberately assume that burden of history without being born into it." I suppose I have been wrestling with that answer ever since.

The late C. Kilmer Myers used to tell the story of Emma, a survivor of the Holocaust, who regularly at 4:00 P.M. each day came to stand outside his church on the lower east side of Manhattan and scream imprecations at Jesus. Finally one day, Kim went down to the street and said to Emma, "Why don't you go inside and tell him?" She disappeared into the church. After an hour had passed, Kim, worried, went in after her. He found Emma, prostrate under the rood, absolutely still. Reaching down, he touched her shoulder. She looked up at him with tears in her eyes and said quietly, "After all, he was a Jew, too."

In his book, *Night*, Elie Wiesel explores the death of his God in the story of the hanging of an "angel-faced" child in the concentration camp in which they both were prisoner.

For more than half an hour he stayed there, struggling between life and death, dying in slow agony under our eyes. And we had to look him full in the face. He was still alive when I passed in front of him. His tongue was still red, his eyes were not yet glazed.

Behind me I heard the same man asking:

"Where is God now?"

And I heard a voice within me answer him:

"Where is He? Here He is—He is hanging here on this gallows. . . ."

The word "holocaust" in Hebrew scripture refers to a whole burnt offering. In early Hebrew religion, the holocaust was a royal sacrifice, a petitionary sacrifice, made by a king at the beginning of his reign or before going into battle. It was a costly meal shared with God that signified God's sharing in human experience.

It was also associated with fire from heaven, a sign that a sacrifice was pleasing to God. Thus fire passed through the halves of Abram's sacrifice during his desert wanderings, called as he was out of all that was familiar to go into the Promise; fire fell from heaven to consume Gideon's sacrifice when he saw the Face of God and did not die; fire fell on David's offering when he saw the angel with the flaming sword. Fire fell on Elijah's altar when he mocked the priests of Baal, and finally, with chariots and horses, on Elijah himself, so full was his life with God's.

One of the most vivid contemporary accounts of the Holocaust was in the first episode of the television series by that name. But the fire this time did not fall from heaven but was lit of men by the hands of men.

During a pogrom in a Russian village, Jews were herded together and taken to the outskirts of town to their wooden synagogue. There the men were forced inside, while the women were huddled together and made to watch as soldiers spread gasoline around the building and ignited it. As the flames began to leap and crackle, the sound of chanting came from within. The men, led by their rabbi, were singing the *Kaddish*, the prayers for the dead—which include the praise of God even in the face of death—for themselves.

The soldiers' act was genocidal and blasphemous, but by singing the *Kaddish*, the burning men transformed their own lives into the essence of a holocaust sacrifice: an incomprehensible whole burnt offering to which the helpless victims mysteriously assent of their own free will even in the midst of the flames.

I don't pretend to understand their offering, nor do I pretend to understand the mystery of the whole offering of God come to us as gift and crucified. Yet the two—the twentieth-century Holocaust and the first-century holocaust and all similar events before and since—are somehow related.

That we will not be able to comprehend these events until the consummation of all things is self-evident. Yet that phrase, "the consummation of all things," implies that even now, at the end of what we call time, all creation has the choice of assent through mortality to be a sacrifice of praise and thanksgiving.

For us Christians, the word "consume" has nuances of eucharistic sacrifice. Bread is consumed. Wine is consumed. Each of these elements in its preparation is holocaust. Grain is ground whole and passes through the fire. Wine, too: in Europe, the harvest is known as "The Passion of the Grape." The whole fruit is crushed, and in the fermentation process, which generates great amounts of heat, the components of juice-becoming-wine are completely broken down and recombined, the wine pressed out from the grape skins and buried in the tomb of a barrel.

Consecrated with them, sharing a meal with God made of the costly offering of the divine life and our lives commingled, we consume this God-given, human-crafted holocaust, our bodies absorbing them by the same oxidation process, so that we may share Christ's self-immolation and indwelling.

There is a relationship between offerer and gift, between priest and sacrifice, that is older than Elijah, older than David, older than Gideon, older than the levitical regulations and definitions. "You shall be my kingdom of priests," says God in Exodus 19, "my holy nation."

It is the whole nation that is to serve as the chosen mediator through which God reveals the unmediated glory that transfigures creation by the divine self-offering. This relationship of sacrifice and priesthood is highly mutable: the offerer necessarily becomes the sacrifice, the holocaust. In Jesus the Christ we see priest and sacrifice becoming inseparable. We see more clearly our responsibility for cocreation with the humble God, and its cost. In the mystical Body—not only the church but all to whom ancient Israel mediates blessing and healing—the effects of this inseparability take on a terrifying aspect.

Are modern holocausts merely a collective unleashing of evil that dwells within the depths of every human being? I do not know.

Is our awareness of the need to "never forget" that ghastly decade of human history, and the visitation of its sins on the present generation, a faint glimmer of the redemptive power of sacrifice to wound our hearts? I do not know.

Can it be not only that these fires were "acceptable"—in the old and very questionable language that implies an arrogant and controlling tyrant of a god in need of appeasement—but that the God who is committed to suffer with and in creation was also willingly consumed in those ovens? I do not know, but I repent in dust and ashes.

Sacrifice by fire is sacrifice of praise and thanksgiving. In the twelfth chapter of the Letter to the Hebrews, we are reminded that we stand before

> Mount Zion and the city of the living God, heavenly Jerusalem, before myriads of angels, the full concourse and assembly of the first-born citizens of heaven, and God the judge of all, and the spirits of good men made perfect, and Jesus the mediator of a new covenant, whose sprinkled blood has better things to tell than the blood of Abel. See that you do not refuse to hear the voice that speaks. . . . Let us therefore give thanks to God, and so worship as God would be worshipped, with reverence and awe; for our God is a consuming fire.

It is *now* that we are standing there; *now* that by our baptism we share both sacrifice and offering with Christ indwelling; *now* that Israel and Israel-by-adoption have the potential to be mediators of blessing and healing to all creation. But the task is hardly accomplished The

82

same chapter reminds us—we who are forty years beyond the Holocaust, we who know it only by repute, we who try to ignore new acts of genocide, to deny the darkness within—"not to lose heart and grow faith. In your struggle against sin you have not yet resisted to the point of shedding your blood."

Most commentaries suggest that this passage refers to martyrdom in the arena. But it also brings to mind the agony in the Garden of Gethsemani, the agony our lives reflect as we attempt to listen to the voice that speaks against the desire to pander to our egos, our selfish appetites, our laziness and apathy, and the potential for wickedness that lurks in our depths, the warfare in which all of us, without exception, are engaged in our Christian vocation.

Today, in the midst of our uneasy culture that appears to be dominated by casual brutality, military corruption, life cheapened by the lust for control over its every aspect, and the destruction of the biosphere, we are still confronted with outward and visible signs of an immense inward and spiritual grace, a gift of the Holy Spirit, which is the possibility to choose to *let go.*

Our letting go, particularly of the wish to isolate and elevate ourselves by controlling and scapegoating others, is a small part of this offering. It is a holocaust of greed and security, things familiar and therefore safe, concepts of self, of how things ought to be and never will, of how they might have been.

They are offered so that through the ashes of silence and weeping, grace can enter, enabling us to discover the joy of cocreating with God a genuinely new order that transfigures in dimensions far beyond our space-time, and without which life on earth as we know it will die from the consequences of our short-sighted choices. Like Abram we go out from the illusion of security into the desert where fire falls from heaven.

All our world becomes Abram's desert, not only because to survive we must learn to live more simply, and by living more simply we discover what fulfillment means, but also because truly simple lives, wherever we live them, are possible only when we realize that it is our dust that engages the Source, not the images we present to the world of commerce. In the humility of our wanderings we are called to fill each place with prayer that is valid, and then let it go; to make each step, each moment, a holocaust of prayer, praise, thanksgiving, that is then let go. This is the heart of prayer, the cry of the heart that has emptied itself of everything most precious to it—even its own idea of itself and its god—so that it may be filled with the fire of the living God.

We are all journeying into the wilderness of faith, and we are all given the hidden gift of Abraham: to go into the promise, into the vows we have made in baptism, called out of all that is familiar; to bless God for the journey and for spacious unknowing; to bless, finally, even our own death.

Our incomplete selves, baptized or not, are touched with fire from heaven, for when we repent of our evil choices, we quite literally come to our selves, God hallows our offering, and we begin to understand that what is unreasonable is that we have so little to offer. We begin to realize that our offering is holy because we make it with Christ indwelling, for the sake of the transfiguration of creation—fragmented and charred to be sure, but with Love's delight. And living, because *anyone*, baptized or not, who makes this offering, with full consciousness or by instinct, passes through death into life everlasting.

We often think of Eucharist as bringing sacred time into linear time. Sometimes it is more fruitful to think of Eucharist as gathering linear time into the sacred, for this is the movement of our true priestly offering in each moment of time.

Astrophysics offers a metaphor that illustrates this incarnate, sacramental glimpse into God's all-time. We can liken sacramental movement to the gravitational force of a black hole, a collapsed star, an infinitely mutable event where everything becomes compressed and intensified. We are drawn through its singularity, the wormhole or time warp where all laws break down. This singularity connects the black hole to its counterpart, a white hole that is infinitely expanding, through which we are expelled into the new creation.

We are drawn to the holocaust, the Host, and we are changed not only by the consecrated Bread and Wine but by the eucharistic offering of each life, by lives and deaths around us, by lives and deaths in our own lives, not only major dislocations and new beginnings, but also small deaths, our hurting of each other and forgiving of each other. Having passed through death and resurrection, we are expelled into the world to transfigure with God's infinitely expanding love.

For all the inexorability of our mortality, we still have to choose: to listen to the fantasies that ravel deeper into anger, resentment, and hate, or to change and grow, to struggle to adore, to face the phantasms of our own evil propensities, propensities that would prevent our offering, prevent sacrifice. And in this sacrifice we persist until our solitude becomes an intensification of the world of cruelty, hunger, poverty, and despair; an Israel wrestling with the God whom we will not let go, and who will not let us go until we receive the fire from heaven that makes us a sacrifice for creation's healing, blessing, and joy.

We are victims of Mercy.

Catherine of Sienna put it this way: "Just as in the Old Testament when sacrifice was offered to God, a fire came and drew to himself the sacrifice that was acceptable to him, so gentle Truth did that to the soul. He sent the fiery mercy of the Holy Spirit and seized the sacrifice of desire that he had made of herself to him."

How do I understand holocaust, any holocaust? I don't. I hope to spend the rest of my life exploring the awful knowledge of humanity as priest and sacrifice, persecutor and victim, executioner and savior.

With François Mauriac, the language of my response dissolves into the silence of weeping:

> And I, who believe that God is love, what answers could I give my young questioner, whose dark eyes still held the reflection of that angelic sadness which had appeared one day upon the face of the hanged child? What did I say to him? Did I speak of that other Israeli, his brother who may have resembled him—the Crucified, whose Cross has conquered the world? Did I affirm that the stumbling block to his faith was the cornerstone of mine, and the conformity between the Cross and the suffering of men was in my eyes the key to that impenetrable mystery whereon the faith of his childhood had perished?

. . . We do not know the worth of one single drop of blood, one single tear. All is grace. If the Eternal is the Eternal, the last word for each of us belongs to Him. This is what I should have told this Jewish child. But I could only embrace him, weeping.

Thus, having uttered what I do not understand, things too wonderful for me, now in the hope of seeing God with my own eyes, I melt away; I become one with these ashes, and repent.

Make us holocaust for your people
pure channels for your love;
send your Holy Spirit to enflame our hearts,
and receive us into the fire of your life.

August
Big Sur Diptych II: Vigil of the Transfiguration
༺༻

Star Fox

❧

On the way to the water pipe yesterday evening I saw a lynx; he saw me, too, and slunk quickly off into the brush at the left side of the road where a grocery store of quail and wood rats awaited his leisurely selection.

I filled my jugs and heard crashing in the woods above; deer, from the sound of it. I went a little up the road, set my jugs down to rest, watched, and waited. The crashing began again. A doe appeared, slipped noisily down to the road, and began to eat at the edge, seeming indifferent, but checking things out for her fawn.

Impatient fawn leaps lightly down to road, frisking. His back is to me, but doe sees and watches with dark eyes, ears twitching. I am upwind so I know she has my scent, yet she is unafraid. After a moment she leans down for another mouthful and I quietly pick up my jugs to leave these two in peace. They watch but do not start, do not panic. I am blessed.

Four A.M. and a broad-bottomed coon wakes me up, raiding my stores. I shine my light on him and he scuttles off into bushes, soon comes back. I chunk a clod of dirt after him and wait under the wheeling bowl of stars to see if he will return again.

A meteor shoots overhead. We are in the month of major star showers. This one is bright and yellow and goes from east to west.

And suddenly I see the fox, also moving east to west. I hold my breath: he trails stars from his tail as he floats along, soundlessly, no sound I can hear.

He pauses, dances even in his stillness. He calls down Aries the warrior and tames him: no war, only music and fire. He calls down the great star Aldebaran from the constellation of the bull (how well I know the bull!), and fire strikes the earth. He laughs with the Pleiades, those shy maidens you can see only if you look from the corner of your eye. Look at them directly and they recede; look at them through binoculars and each shines brighter than Aldebaran, even the shyest.

Fox, little fox, there are no sour grapes or sweet for you here, only light, starlight, stars' dust, clouds of unknowing, but to you they are known. It is we with our names and intuitions who must grope. You flicker down the heavenly spheres bringing the whole population of the universe in your wake: centaur and scorpion, warrior and maiden, hunter and starry game. But there is no plunder of centaurs, no sting of scorpions, no rape of maiden by warrior, no killing of game by hunter.

You carry us, little fox, into this assembly; you help us seek the Maker of the Pleiades and Orion, you carry them to us. We wheel and dance; we plunge into the darkness and are dazzled with the light. We know deep darkness becomes morning, and wonder at the stars' greater brightness as first light's sheer and gauzy veil slips over the eastern ridge.

Star fox, little swift, trailing starlight and constellations, forgive our heaviness, forgive our clay feet. Tell our Maker that we too would dance in the darkness and desert, we too would have your lightness and grace. Say, O little one of large eyes and huge ears, that we would see the Face unveiled and hear the whispered Voice. Speak for us: our words are clumsy, our eyes blurred, our hearing dulled.

Speak for us: we are dancers, singers; we trail fire in our hearts as we hurtle through space-time. Your eyes glow in the starlight and you look into our hearts and know; your ears move receptively, you hear our pleas, feel our longing, bear the Seeker in the dark.

But tonight, this moonless night of music and ever-changing, never-changing dance, speak for us, hear for us, dance for us, bring us into the starry company, bring them to us . . .

Lightning in the East

-&

Awake from sodden sleep. Drugged with dreams from Bosch that sneak into the bushes as consciousness makes half-hearted return.

The night is getting warm. I went to bed in a flannel nightgown; it and my sleeping bag are soaked with sweat.

My left sinus hurts. Hurts with an ache sharp and dull and full all at once, sure sign of changing pressure.

Change. Something is happening.

I inch out of my damp cocoon and zip open the tent flap.

Twenty-three hundred feet below, muffling the surf, glimmering in the moonless night, is a bed of fog. Silly with sleep I contemplate a swan-dive and bouncing on it.

Then I wake up fast. There is lightning in the east. It dulls the stars when it explodes; they seem brighter when it is gone. I sense rather than hear the rumble of thunder. It comes through the mountain rock that stirs uneasily with pressure that both rises and falls. The water in its heart is summoned by the water from heaven falling in torrents on the valley to the southeast.

The stars seem caught in their motion, motionless. The temperature rises. The fog rises. It is both hotter and colder. Somewhere on this mountain, heat and cold will meet; somewhere fire and water.

I am caught and cower. Earth trembles toward dawn as lightning etches ridges in sharp relief. All is hushed in waiting, all exhausted in tension. Little by little the fog creeps up the mountain. Sharper and brighter lightning flashes in the east.

Cry to the mountains, "Fall on us!" and to the hills, "Hide us!"

Who can bear this tearing polarity; who can arc between fire and water, rock and bread, tears and wine? Who can stand a heart riven by darkling light; who can endure molten Love coursing through the earth?

A line of fire stretches from heaven to meet fog rising from the sea. What will be released in this elemental meeting? What energy from polarity? What mutation from collision?

I am caught halfway up, halfway down; I am caught between heaven and earth; I am caught by fire that speaks to fire indwelling and water that calls to my tears. I arc to meet the lightning and embrace the mercy of fog to cool my burns.

Star Fox and Red Bull swirl in the Dance; psalm-singers without number charge the silence with music no mortal ear can hear and live. The lines of fog and fire draw closer.

Who are we, O Fiery Name, that you are mindful of us? Who are we that you should make us a meeting place of these contraries, torn between earth and heaven? Who are we that through us fire should erupt from creation and cleanse all things, that Beauty should return in her fullness, that star should marry sea and Peace kiss each one upon the lips?

The stars bend low. "Tonight?" I ask, longing through my fear, is it tonight? Star and fire and fog, the weight too much and nothing . . . nothing . . .

A little breeze rustles dried husks of wild oats, seed long fallen into the ground to wait for winter rains. Its sighing is my longing; the husks my food until I am consumed, grain planted and ground, leavened and broken. Sunrise dulls the stars; lightning fades; fog recedes. Star Fox and Red Bull sleep until the Feast of Feasts . . .

And yet . . . and yet . . . how is the sorrowing earth not transfigured this night? How is this sowing of fire not sparked, arced through our clay this night, this morning, this darkness and light both alike?

Time is our foolish booth in which we try to trap what has begun and ended and even now is borne in us. We are blind because we see, but it is in the cloud that envelops and leaves us senseless that we know a little Truth, dimly, stupidly, and return home rejoicing, not believing, yet hoping . . .

91

Sun burns its way into the morning, burns our staring eyes, burns us into new life of another day. We break bread at sun's zenith, cry, "O Christ come quickly!" Under sun beg for Sun; broken-hearted fed with Bread broken, hearts pierced with light too great to bear, burst asunder with all creation pouring out from each in floodlife, fountains, streams, rivers from stoneheartflesh, molten, living stones.

September

Intercession

Open our eyes to see you;
open our ears to hear you;
open our hearts to know you.

There are as many approaches to intercession as there are people.

Churches often publish and distribute a regular cycle of prayer. Some people keep elaborate notebooks, crammed with names and intentions. Catherine Doherty wrote that she kept such a notebook beneath an icon of Our Lady, and she was sure the Blessed Virgin read that book to her Son every night.

One day I visited Washington Cathedral in the company of a seven-year-old boy who asked what the rack of candles in the Chapel of the Holy Spirit was all about. I told him and helped him light a candle of his own. A Cistercian abbot has a huge poster of Our Lady of Guadalupe in his office and beneath it is a cup where he puts slips of paper with names and intentions. In *Letters to Malcolm*, C. S. Lewis tells us that he asked God to care for "the lady on the train," or "the old crock in the greengrocer's," or something like that. But God understands.

Once I read that Carthusians use no names at all because, the author rather nastily remarked, they don't want to ruin the purity of their prayer. Well, the Carthusians may be on to something, but I suspect the man who wrote that remark doesn't understand what he is seeing any more than the tourists in the Syrian and Egyptian deserts understood what they saw. They twisted their accounts in such a way that the meaning of the lives of the solitaries became distorted into an ancient *Guinness Book of Records*, instead of communicating the struggle for purity of heart as the transfiguration of ordinary lives by the Mercy of God.

Now, just as it is folly to say, "Notebook keepers are better than Carthusians," or "This technique of prayer is better than that," or to presume to judge or evaluate prayer—to say, "This was good prayer," or "This was a higher form of prayer," as if we could know how God receives our prayer, or escape the self-regard hidden in such evaluations—so it is equally foolish to impose an artificial form of intercession on ourselves just because others say it is the correct thing to do.

Yet I think we have to ask the question, What is it we do when we intercede?

First of all, we have to realize we're not always at our best. We have to pray what we are able to pray. Sometimes this can be very primitive.

A long time ago when I was living in Manhattan, I spent a lot of time trying to kill the prayer that kept rising in me like an unwanted gas bubble in a twenty-loaf blob of bread dough. I finally came to realize that my efforts to push it down and deny its existence were futile, but at the same time, I was very frightened of being overwhelmed if I did stop fighting it. I asked a friend what I should do.

"Oh," he said, "use it to pray for things like taxicabs when you need them. If it makes you feel safer, don't ask God for them, but pray to something inanimate like a fire hydrant."

So I spent the next few weeks experimenting with this technique. Whenever I was late for an appointment, I prayed to the nearest fire hydrant for a cab.

The results were amazing.

Taxis would appear from nowhere. If ten people along the curb were signalling for cabs, the only one that appeared would stop in front of me. I could get taxis at rush hour. I could get taxis in the rain. I could get taxis at rush hour in the rain on the Friday of a three-day weekend!

By the time God decided this joke had gone on long enough and sent me the Dark Night of the Taxicab, I was still frightened, but also a little more ready to let go my illusory control over prayer. (I might add that since that time I have never been able to get taxis in New York.)

We have to pray where we are and what we can. And we shouldn't try to fool ourselves: intercession is hard work. We are lazy about it and avoid it for very good reasons. Prayer, especially intercession, is warfare. Prayer is death. As we pray we fast; as we pray we die: we have to deny ourselves everything else in our lives and just *do* it.

What are we doing when we intercede? Often in our heart of hearts we seem to be trying to manipulate God, as if God were a Controller to be controlled, or as if we had to beg God to reconsider what seems to be a poorly contrived *fait accompli*. The ancient Romans used the word "intercede" to mean "interposing a veto." We often seem to be trying to veto what we wrongly perceive as God's intervention, to wheedle and bargain, standing over and against what seems to be the rigid course we mistakenly perceive as "God's will." This tyrant-god is human projection, not the God of Sinai rooted in the stable and open reciprocity of Covenant. This is the capricious deity who needs to be pleased and placated, not the loving God whose wisdom and judgment are given from the perspective of crucifixion and resurrection.

This false stereotype of God is prevalent today because, like the fire hydrant, it is safe. If we can confine God to our own categories, to our own safe boundaries and concepts, we know what we're dealing with. God won't ask too much of us; we won't be overwhelmed.

I don't think God rejects this sort of prayer; I don't think God rejects any prayer. God understands. And when I catch myself in a primitive attitude, trying to control God as if God weren't indwelling and suffering within the creation, as if God were a safe and closed system, I imagine I catch a glimmer of divine amusement.

But intercessory prayer is *not* safe, not if we choose to enter into it in a deeper way. Intercession, like all other kinds of prayer, is really a form of adoration, and the farther we move into it, the more likely we are to forget ourselves, our ideas, our desires in the Face of light and love.

What we cannot comprehend of pain and suffering is often an invitation to enlarge our hearts. The image of the lady with the alabaster box is appropriate here. We are the lady; our hearts are made of stone and sealed like tombs. When they are broken open, God pours love through us onto the Body, which is one another and all creation.

Sometimes, through fear or rage or sin, the box snaps shut—maybe on our fingers—and we are left struggling to find the key that will open it again. Paradoxically, the key to unlock it can be intercession. The access to Love is love. Or, put another way, when we feel incapable of entering directly into the pure love of God, we can make ourselves available to it by tangible love, by holding someone dear to us in that Love.

Anthony Bloom describes this approach in *Courage to Pray*. He refers to the late Staretz Silouan of Mount Athos. "Let us be encouraged," Bloom writes, "by the story of the monk who was praying for his neighbours and who gradually lost consciousness of this earth because he became so wrapped up in God, and who found all his neighbours again in God."

Often we pray for people by their given names but, like C. S. Lewis, I'm forgetful of names and I, too, refer God to "the man in the hardware store" or "the child feeding the swans." But, again, God understands. The name God hears is not a name given by humans but the secret name on the white stone bestowed by God's creative and sustaining love.

Though we may think we "refer" people to God, or bring them to God's attention, what we are really doing—for God needs no reminding—is creating possibility, opening and offering ourselves to be used in whatever way God and the other person deem appropriate. Do we dare accept the invitation to enter the coming-into-being of another? And, conversely, do we dare ask a friend, or the saints, to enter our coming-to-be? Do we dare ask God to pray the saints for us, to allow them to share with us the love of God, poured out through their own peculiar brokenness by which the Word is spread abroad in our world? It's a terrifying prospect.

But this offering, this sacrifice, is the priestly vocation of our baptism by which the love of God becomes incarnate through our lives willingly made sacrament. To make ourselves available to the mystery of creation is to enter the darkness of unknowing.

One of our fears is that we will be changed by what we pray. We run the risk of being burnt up, of being holocaust for one another. Sometimes we become aware—perhaps visualized, perhaps not—of actually being with the person we are praying for: walking down the street with a friend or stranger; watching a surgical procedure and at the same time lying on the table, sustaining the other's breath; sitting in a small, dim room with someone near despair; holding a sick child.

Once such an experience came unbidden as I sat down for evening meditation. An airliner had crashed that day, and prayer for the crew and passengers pushed aside all else. There was a vivid sense of being in the plane's cabin among them in their agony as they fell toward earth. This sequence was repeated over and over during the next half hour, as if the prayer itself required my enduring those terrible moments. Experiences like this one should not be sought, nor can prayer be evaluated by their presence or absence, but the prayer of entering-in may open us to unlooked-for, sometimes frightening awareness.

In *Descent into Hell*, Charles Williams describes entering-in as the doctrine of substituted love. Stanhope, who is choosing to live this prayer, is talking to a girl who keeps meeting a doppelgänger, a vision of herself. She is very afraid.

"To bear a burden is precisely to carry it instead of," said Stanhope. "If you're still carrying yours, I'm not carrying it for you—however sympathetic I may be. And anyhow, there's no need to introduce Christ, unless you wish. It's a fact of experience. If you give a weight to me, you can't be carrying it for yourself; all I'm asking you to do is to notice that blazing truth. It doesn't sound very difficult."

"And if I could," she said. "If I could do—whatever it is you mean, would I? Would I push my burden on to anybody else?"

"Not if you insist on making a universe for yourself," he answered. "If you want to disobey and refuse the laws that are common to us all, if you want to live in pride and division and anger, you can. But if you will be part of the best of us, and laugh and be ashamed with us, then you must carry someone else's burden. I haven't made the universe, and it isn't my fault. But I'm sure that this is a law of the universe, and not to give up your parcel is quite as much to rebel as not to carry another's. You'll find it quite easy if you let yourself do it."

Then Stanhope gives the girl his instructions:

"When you are alone," he said, "remember that I am afraid instead of you, and that I have taken over every kind of worry. Think merely that; say to yourself—'he is being worried,' and go on. Remember it is mine. If you do not see it, well; if you do, you will not be afraid ... because you will leave all that to me."

Even more solemn is the intercession of actual substitution—the offering of ourselves instead of—which, if we stop to think about it, is probably the most appalling form of intercessory prayer. It is most definitely the response to a call, an invitation, and not lightly undertaken. Bloom describes such a substitution in an encounter between two women during the Russian civil war.

In a small provincial village that had just changed hands, a young woman of twenty-seven or so was trapped with her two small children. Her husband belonged to the opposite side. She had been unable to escape in time, and she was in hiding, trying to save her own and her children's lives. She spent a day and a night in great fear and the following evening the door of her hiding place was opened and a young woman, a neighbour of her own age, came in. She was a simple woman with nothing extraordinary about her. She said, "Is So and So your name?" The mother replied, "Yes," in great fear. The neighbour said, "You have been discovered; they are coming for you tonight to shoot you. You must leave." The mother looked at her children and said, "Where shall I go? How can I get away with these children? They could not walk fast enough or far enough for us not to be caught." And this neighbour suddenly became a neighbour in the full sense of the gospel. She approached the mother and said with a smile, "They will not go after you because I will stay here in your place." The mother must have said, "They will shoot you." She replied, "Yes, but I have no children. You *must* leave." And the mother went.

Substitution also occurs in the realm of pure prayer, but in this mystery we must yield entirely to the love of Christ praying in us in ways far beyond knowing.

There is no way to judge and evaluate intercession. God knows the secrets of our hearts and is able to work in and through us when we are least aware of it, often when our prayer seems most useless and insipid, or when we're not aware of praying at all. Rarely are we allowed a glimpse, or given reassurance. God is wise to give us dry rations, because in our frailty we would quickly begin to pray for consolations for ourselves, instead of breaking free of our inhibitions and away from safe fire hydrants to participate in Love.

It is this participation to which the Letter to the Colossians refers when it speaks of making up what is lacking in the sufferings of Christ. Though Christ's humility has triumphed, we have, by our baptism, committed ourselves in that humble Love to the battles still raging with cosmic powers of darkness.

So whether we intercede like notebook keepers or like Carthusians, we need to be aware that we are leaving ourselves wide open to be used in some unknowable way. If we feel forgotten, left out, or unheard, we should not give up, for God has sent Light and Truth to lead us to Love's holy hill and dwelling.

Glory to God whose power working in us
can do infinitely more than we can ask or imagine;
glory from generation to generation in the church
and in Christ Jesus for ever and ever.

October
❧❧❧

All Hallows Eve

Almighty God, give us grace to cast away the works of darkness,
and put on the armor of light, now in the time of this mortal life
in which your Son Jesus Christ came
to visit us in great humility;
that in the last day, when he shall come again in his glorious
majesty to judge both the living and the dead,
we may rise to the life immortal.

One cool October evening, I put on my sweater and sandals, flicked on the porch lamp, and went outside into the moist autumn air to go to a Eucharist at the church across the way. My eyes adjusted enough to see the wooden steps, but beyond the edge of the light were shadows, and I had to trust the memory of my feet for the stone flight going up the hill.

As I stepped out into the dark, there was a tearing shriek, a noise like rubbing your wet hand over the surface of a tightly blown-up balloon, or the friction of tires against the road when you jam on the brakes.

I looked down and saw a half-dead blue jay, one of the cats' offerings, bloody evidence of a hope that the gift of this delicate morsel would convince me I should relent and allow the donor to become the solitary's official cat.

Ugh.

My 140 pounds had squeezed a column of air out of the bird's four-ounce body through its constricted throat. That was what made the noise. Though I doubt the bird was still alive, its body under my gaze stirred with faint neurological twitchings. I hurriedly dispatched it, threw it out into the blackness toward the leaf-pit, and with hollow helplessness in my stomach, made my way over to the Eucharist.

During the Liturgy, a question revolved continually in my mind: Why, why by our very existence must we involuntarily damage others? It's bad enough to have the capacity for willful sin. And at the Offertory was all the groaning and travail of creation.

I have been haunted by this question for many years, especially as it concerns the relationships of human beings one with another. I will never forget the day I first understood what older spiritual writers call "instant mutual antipathy," that there are people in this world who will damage me and whom I will damage not by doing anything, but simply by existing.

For some people, to be intimidating to others is to live with an exhilarating sense of power. But for me, in every encounter of this nature, I experience deep shame, humiliation, pain, self-loathing, and grief. I have come to believe that this fact of human relationships lies at the root of what is often called original sin, which we tend to shrug off as something we can't do much about.

Often when we talk about the Fall we speak in nervously jocular terms, like the end man in a minstrel show, retelling the story of de snake who gave Eve de apple, who ate and gave to Adam, and when de Lawd God walked in de garden in de cool of de evening and asked Adam where he was and what he had done, Adam pointed to Eve, Eve to de snake, and de snake, he lay low.

This reading from Genesis frequently inspires uneasy laughter, a laughter that flies in the face of phantasms flickering at the edges of our vision, a pervasive miasma of the resonances of evil choices that penetrates our defenses and tries to influence every choice.

October's end is the season of ghoulies and ghosties, long-leggety beasties, and things that go bump in the night, the season when we trivialize the horror of the vaguely known or, worse, try by psychologizing to dismiss the ghastly propensities that live in the depths of our own hearts, biding their time, waiting for their chance.

Maybe we try to tell ourselves that this is the only season of the year when familiars emerge, that, for one night, we can let them out to play without too much risk, knowing that bells heralding the morning of saints and souls will drive these wraiths back underground, much like Disney's vision of the night on Bald Mountain.

Oh no.

Oh no.

This is the delusion the Evil One would have us take as truth, that it doesn't really exist, that it is a neurosis, a bad case of indigestion, or a child's night-terror.

You may scoff. You may ask on a note of incredulity, "Do you really believe that old stuff?"

And dread will press on my heart:

Oh yes.

Oh yes.

I believe.

And perhaps you will say with an amused, knowing look, "But how? Why?"

And I will say, "I know. I have seen it. I have heard its cajoling. I have felt its creeping, paralyzing presence."

And you may look at me as if I were quite mad.

And perhaps I am.

But I have seen it: I have seen it in the face of hate, a Vietnamese officer executing a Viet Cong prisoner at point blank range, four feet in front of a news photographer. I have seen it in the face of my older sister in one of our ancient sibling rages. I have looked in the mirror and seen it in my own face.

I have heard it whisper, "Just this once," or "No one will know," or "Self-discipline can be harmful to your psychological health."

I have seen it waiting by my bed as racing, angry, obsessive thoughts wrestle in my consciousness with the Jesus Prayer. And it waits, waits for me to make my choice. Oh yes, I know it well.

And yet within that choice lies the hope of my salvation.

It is no accident that we shutter our houses against principalities and powers the night before we celebrate those saints and souls who endured this warfare in themselves, who died reaching for the Light

104

they glimpsed oblique and veiled, that now bursts in full radiance upon them.

We make heroes of them, and indeed they were. We magnify their deeds, and they were great deeds.

But if we look beyond the fabulous that obscures the humanity of the saints, we see that their deeds sprang from the miracle of Christ's indwelling love, from which all the demons of the universe, all the cosmic powers of evil could not separate them.

We have lost our sense of incarnation. We have debased it to something magical. We have obscured the elemental life of Sacrament, stable-born and crucified, now locked away in golden tabernacles.

We need to recover this elemental life. We need to acknowledge the warfare. We need to see salvation at work in the most fundamental laws of the universe.

I will never forget the summer's day when a friar came home and, catching sight of me as he jumped out of the borrowed yellow VW bug, joyously shouted, "Did you see in the *Times* that the Second Law of Thermodynamics has been challenged?"

The Second Law of Thermodynamics was supposedly (among other things) the scientific refutation of resurrection, the spiritual and cultural depressant of our age. It was the law of entropy. It said that everything in the universe proceeded surely and inexplicably toward chaos and decay. But someone in Europe discovered that out of disintegrating particles and seeming chaos come new and more subtly complex forms, that very rottenness spawns new life. And now we know that great beauty can be created by what seems random and unpredictable.

Since the patterning of particles ultimately is expressed in the patterning of larger forms—plants, birds, cats, humans, planets, galaxies, black holes, and universes—the announcement in the *Times* has vast implications of hope, the sort of hope that makes us doubtful Christians look at each other in relief and bravely say, "I told you so."

Now, you may ask, what does this arcane law of physics have to do with ghoulies and ghosties, with Sacrament and saints?

Simply this: that embracing the incomprehensible pain of fang and claw, guarding the shades of the Evil One, transforming the deadly propensities dwelling in us, is a Love that enfolds pain, casts down Evil, and purifies our hearts. That far from understanding creation as having fallen once for all, it is still falling, just as it is still being set free.

Prayer can be our participation in one another's bringing-into-being. But this participation is not confined to intercession. It is the prayer of enduring what lives within and around us, the prayer of our lives' choices that at every moment create resonances that either gather and strengthen evil or bring into being the spaciousness of the kingdom where there is no pain or death, and where God's suffering in Jesus who is the Christ wipes away every tear from every eye.

And where we see face to Face.

He who gives this testimony speaks, "Yes, I am coming soon!"

Amen, even so, *maranatha*, come quickly Christ Jesus!

November

Kontakion

The sons of the prophets who were at Jericho drew near to Elisha and said to him, "Do you know that today the Lord will take away your master from over you?" And he answered, "Yes, I know it; hold your peace."

Then Elijah said to him, "Tarry here, I pray you; for the Lord has sent me to the Jordan." But he said, "As the Lord lives and as you yourself live, I will not leave you." ... Then Elijah took his mantle, and rolled it up, and struck the water, and the water was parted to the one side and to the other, until the two of them could go over on dry ground.

When they had crossed, Elijah said to Elisha, "Ask what I shall do for you before I am taken from you." And Elisha said, "I pray you, let me inherit a double share of your spirit." And he said, "You have asked a hard thing; yet if you see me as I am being taken from you, it shall be so for you; but if you do not see me, it shall not be so." And as they still went on and talked, behold, a chariot of fire and horses of fire separated the two of them. And Elijah went up by a whirlwind into heaven. And Elisha saw it and he cried, "My father, my father! The chariots of Israel and its horsemen!" And he saw him no more.

Then he took hold of his own clothes and rent them in two pieces. And he took up the mantle of Elijah that had fallen from him, and went back and stood on the bank of the Jordan. Then he took the mantle of Elijah that had fallen from him and struck the water, saying, "Where is the Lord, the God of Elijah?" And when he had struck the water, the water was parted to one side and to the other; and Elisha went over.

When the Franciscan friar who was very much a spiritual father to me died, he left his sons and daughters a portion of his mantle. And for some weeks and months after his death, I lashed the water with that mantle and called upon his God. I did a lot of growing up.

We seem to grow at different rates. Each of us has a rhythm. And within each of us are different rhythms: our bodies grow at one rate, our psyches by complex processes, our souls even more mysteriously. Yet we are really one fabric being woven by a master Weaver who knows that the most beautiful cloth is that in which the flaws, mistakes, and gaps are preserved and integrated into the finished work.

Our bodies grow comparatively rapidly. By the time we are twenty or so, they are complete, as complete as they will ever be, and from the age of twenty-five, the downhill slide begins. Our psyches and especially our souls are a different matter. By the time we are twenty, our psyches have just begun to cope with the unimaginably vast amounts of conscious and unconscious material that is our own peculiar formative environmental stew, spiced with the unique genetic material each of us is given.

Most of us come out of adolescence with burning energy, expressed partly as unfocused anger or rage, partly as the creative drive that will focus our lives into some sort of coherent whole, and partly as a deep unconscious groping that will keep us searching to the end for the God who is both indwelling and familiar, yet far beyond knowing.

Years ago I had a friend, a lady, one of the last of the great ladies in the old manner, a member of the fabled New York 400, whose legendary parties, mad antics, and elegant disdain for convention gave Manhattan its romantic mystique. In a family with three astonishingly beautiful sisters, in an age that doted on the exquisite, she was physically the ugly duckling. Undaunted by her body's liabilities, she became a deeply loving and beloved doyenne of New York society, and her generous public and secret charitable work galvanized her envious peers, whose characters did not improve with the natural deterioration of their porcelain faces. She finally married when she and her husband were in their fifties.

When I knew her, she had been crippled by arthritis for two decades but remained indomitable. Only in the last few years of her life did she slow down a little, not being able to manage shipboard travel any longer, but still solicitous of her charities and her tyrannical husband's every childish whim.

He, at ninety-one, had never grown up. Having come from a Prussian family where a nanny tied his shoes, he felt it was unreasonable to learn to do that, though he mastered the intricacies of the stock market at an early age. There are different ways of being a child.

This friend of mine, who was herself nearing ninety, confided to me once on a mellow evening, "Don't be fooled, dearie. It's only our bodies that grow old, and inside I'm still a young girl who dances until dawn."

Wisdom, wisdom born of love and suffering is a gift that comes from and with the God we seek. My spiritual father had that wisdom; others who have been spiritual parents to me have it. But if you mentioned wisdom to any of these people, they would regard you with irony, knowing theirs to be but a fragment, or unaware that what to them seems commonplace is wisdom to others.

Growing up is hard.

For us late bloomers it takes most of our twenties for grief over hubris and callowness to burn most of the rage out of us and to make us painfully aware of how careful we must be. We go from feeling that no one pays attention or listens to us to realizing the tremendous, sometimes terrifying impact that our words, actions, and, yes, our prayers have on others. The beginning, gnawing knowledge of just who we are—the price of our forgivenness—ceases being a source of rebellion and becomes a welcome, burning fire, a fire that sears and purifies and yet does not consume.

So much of growing up is letting go: letting go our ideas of what life should be like, for instance. It often takes a long time to let go the conviction that life is or ought to be fair and satisfying according to youthful concepts. That's part of the rage. And rage is grieved out through coming to understand that life will never be fair or what we expect. This is knowledge that comes through disappointment, through loss, through being broken again and again.

After the death of my Franciscan father, childhood, especially my spiritual childhood, melted away like patches of snow under a heavy rain.

One of the hardest things about growing up is that we suddenly find our parents are our children. This happened to me some years before the Franciscan's death. It's a shock. We realize our parents are looking to *us* for solace, for nurturing, and in spite of the illusion we attempt to maintain, the illusion that they are still in charge, each of us knows with the certainty born of long association that the shoe is on the other foot, that the worm has turned.

This is an unrecoverable loss and worth grieving over, but it takes a while. We go through a lot of waste motion testing this new, unsure, sometimes swampy ground to accept the sadness and overcome our disbelief. And then one day something happens (or maybe it isn't even that specific), and the reality of the situation sets in. It's a whole new ball game. (There is always, of course,the sudden rereversal of roles and the wisdom and love that remain—they are still our *parents*. But that's another subject.) And when parents die, the feeling of being without walls or sure touch-points, except the invisible cradling hand of God, is impressed with even more surety.

This reversal of roles can be even more poignant with spiritual parents. When my Franciscan father learned of his illness, our roles subtly began to change. In our fourteen-year relationship, we spoke often of death as the passage we must traverse to fully see the loving Face of God, which desire is the terrible longing that brings us to faith in the first place, and paradoxically makes every moment of life all the more precious.

A year or so before he knew of his final illness, this friar spoke with some amusement of the years he had spent railing at God because he was not taken through the veil sooner—and then, with a little embarrassment at his folly, of resignation to take it at God's pace.

Then he learned he was ill and wrote that he was waiting on the railway station platform to "go home for Christmas," though in the end he had to wait nearly two years before the train arrived. I don't think he ever stopped being impatient with God. When we said our final good-bye, as we stood after he blessed me, I gently teased him.

"Be patient with God. And don't forget me, ever."

And he got that look on his face of amusement, wonder, and

intense love that was so essentially himself, and which I will carry with me for the rest of my life.

With his death, his mantle settled down. A few days passed before the numbness wore off. Then I took that mantle, lashed the water, and called on his God. As prepared as I was for his death, in the end there was no way to prepare for it.

There were other losses in the two-week space after his death. My flaky aunt died. With her died a parenting of the free spirit in me. With her death I was kicked out of the nest to free-fall.

She broke away from a stuffy midwestern family back in the early days of Hollywood, where for forty years she worked for Central Casting. It left its mark: she was a combination of Margaret Rutherford, Bette Davis playing Queen Elizabeth I, and Loretta Young. Although for some reason I never really got to know her until ten years before her death, when we met at my grandfather's funeral, she reinforced, encouraged, and fostered in me, against all family pressure, the deep knowledge that happiness and holiness do not necessarily come with material wealth and power. Now it is my turn to do the fostering, and while one is nurtured by nurturing, it is never quite the same.

During this same two-week period, a very close friend, another Franciscan, was ordained and celebrated his first Eucharist. When he crossed into the mystery of his first consecration, I had an ineffable sense of loss as he began the great and lonely journey that is the privilege and the burden of the person who offers our gathered solitudes in Bread and Wine, united, broken, and sent out.

In retrospect, I know too that what we were experiencing that day was the artificial and illegitimate gulf the church opens between the quality of our offering and his by the debased and debasing attitudes toward the nonordained it continues to hold, and by its implicit message, protestations to the contrary notwithstanding, that only the ordained are really "complete" Christians, capable of making the offering of our lives at the Eucharist. This problem continues to grow, and the objectification of Christ's indwelling sacrifice that it effects drains life and meaning, and fragments our relationship in community.

In retrospect, I know my friend felt this also; in retrospect the mystery is deepened because on that morning we acted together in true Eucharist: his hands shook as he picked up the chalice, and I felt all our hearts and invisible hands leap out to steady his—holding up his arms like Moses'—and sure enough, his hands steadied. But something in his relationship with all of us had quietly, inexorably changed. No matter how good, how beautiful, how holy that moment seemed at the time, there was loss. And we had to let him go.

This last slow shock impressed the reality of role reversal in virtually every relationship: as I grew older, I would ever more frequently be asked to change roles. An older friend reminded me then: *You* are now the older generation. And, as chance would have it, as I prepare this new edition, I am reminded again by the dying from AIDS of my friend whose hands we helped to hold up at that long-ago Eucharist, and which we are holding up again, by prayer and by touch, helping him guide each mouthful of food and each sip of water. And who dares to say this is not Eucharist?

For all of this, I protest like Jeremiah that I am but a child.

But to return to the past: underneath all of these changes, the usual flux at the friary: people going away to begin new work; people coming home having ended work.

Growing up is hard.

Finally I was able to do a lot of weeping. I did most of it in my sleep. In fact, I went to bed for three days, getting up for Offices, Eucharist, and an occasional meal. A wise man had taught me to grieve that way some years before.

But this time it was different. This time instead of using a mere psychological tool, I claimed my inheritance with and in Christ; and, with the inarticulate whispered cry of a child to its Mother, crept under that Wing we pray about every night at Compline, the image of the Spirit's sheltering that appears and reappears in the gospels and psalms.

I crept under the shadow of that Wing and slept, and wept, and with that blessed grieving time, three mornings' long vigils, and a letter from the brother who had been with my Franciscan father during his last moments, the uncontrolled sobbing finally was released. God purified me with tears, and I did a lot of growing up.

I know now that the only way to cope with growing up is to become a little child, to choose to evolve with all our complexity toward simplicity; to accept and trust as a little child trusts, only now with the second innocence born of sin and pain transfigured that is more precious than the first, that enables us to walk into dark corridors knowing we will be clobbered, but walking in anyway; to love wholeheartedly with wonder and astonishment and delight; to not be afraid of a child's self-forgetful absorption in life, approached uncritically and with suspended judgment, so that we may learn true critical discernment.

Grief is indispensable. Jesus knew that. He wept often. He wept at the news of John the Baptist's death; he wept over Lazarus and the blindness of our hearts; he wept over Jerusalem. Grief made him grow. And us. It's really the only emotion we have that can be unmixed in content and motive. It purifies our hearts.

Growing up is hard. But we learn. We learn the nuances of life. We learn, for instance, the difference between depression and desolation.

Depression seems always to have an element of unresolved anger and rebellion in it; desolation is like a forest after a fire has gone through: grief has burned all the anger out, and there is an element of harsh beauty, joy, and even music in its depths.

Depression turns us in on ourselves; desolation intensifies our seeking. The source of depression is often vague; the source of desolation is always specific: it can settle on us not only with a deeper acceptance of solitude, but also after God comes, kindles us into flame, and seems to hide again. Depression has no peace and gives no peace; at the heart of the desolation of the desert is the Peace that passes understanding, the "strife closed in the sod."

Losses of good people, relationships, options, things are worth the grieving. Like Elisha we lash the water, and it is not only the Jordan that parts for us to cross dry-shod to the promised land; it is a river, too, of tears.

So let us pray for ourselves and our childhood as we pray for those who have died, who precede us where there is no more pain or grief, and where every tear is wiped away from every eye.

May we rest in peace.
Alleluia.

❧

Give rest, O Christ, to your servants, with your saints where sorrow and pain are no more, neither sighing, but life everlasting.

You only are immortal, our Creator and Maker; and we are mortal, formed of the earth, and to earth we shall return. For so you did ordain when you created me, saying, "You are dust, and to dust you shall return." All of us go down to the dust; yet even at the grave we make our song: Alleluia, alleluia, alleluia.

Give rest, O Christ, to your servants, with your saints where sorrow and pain are no more, neither sighing, but life everlasting.

December

Solitude

⁓

Our culture shrinks from solitude.

The cults of narcissism and togetherness whisper insidiously that there is something sick about being solitary—which is very different from being alone.

We are all solitaries.

One measure of the distance at which most people hold solitude is the frequent comment, "You don't *look* like a hermit," followed by the query, "What do you *do* in solitude?"

Often I wonder if I'm supposed to have green hair or something, and I'm tempted to reply, "I don't do, I *be*." But in the event, we always seem to end by laughing.

Perhaps there are two questions that underlie this question: Why are people drawn to explore solitude? What is solitude like?

These are unanswerable questions. Each person must try to fathom solitude in the depths of the heart beyond words, images, symbols, analogies. Merton once wrote that all there is to be said about solitude has been said by the wind in the pine trees. This comment seems a bit romantic in view of the volumes he turned out, but we do need to try to articulate our explorations, if only to ourselves, even if in the end our questions dwindle in the Silence.

It may be helpful to make some distinctions and blur others. Solitude entails and is the heart of our engagement with community. Exterior solitude and interior solitude tend to merge with interior silence. On the other hand, you can have physical solitude and not be in solitude at all because you have a cocktail party or disco racketing in your head. At the same time, I've had some very solitary moments on the West Side IRT at rush hour. And interior silence has very little, if anything, to do with whether or not you are talking to people.

One way to respond to the first question about why people are drawn to explore solitude is to look at Jesus and John the Baptist. They went into hiding to come out of hiding, to become bare, exposed, vulnerable, revealed.

Just as surely as John was overjoyed at the appearance of Jesus when these two towering solitudes met on the bank of the River Jordan, so Jesus recognized John's authority as one who had been in the wilderness where he, Jesus, was going. Jesus came to John as an authority, yet John tried to yield to Jesus.

We know why Jesus went into the wilderness: he was led by the Spirit to be tempted by the devil. You can't separate his baptism from his temptation. He was purified, tempted; God spoke to his heart and angels came and ministered to him.

But we are told nothing about John from the time of his first recognition of Jesus in his mother's womb, until his emergence from the desert to point to the Light, the revelation of the Word incarnate. John went into the desert to become empty so he could be filled with and sent by God, to point to the light of God. The evangelist says, "he was not the light but was sent to bear witness to the light, that all might believe through him."

After John's death, Jesus the light refers to John as a lamp. A lamp is filled with light, and the oil that fires the lamp is the oil of repentance. John preached repentance and baptized that people might be prepared for the light.

Why?

Most of us have the experience that love can be unbearable. John must have received it in solitude and baptized to make the One who was coming, Love incarnate, a little easier to bear. Our baptism in the crucified and risen Christ enables us to bear it; we learn to bear each other's love so we can learn to bear God's.

But often when we find love unbearable, we are like the little child in the supermarket having a tantrum, while Mother supports, embraces, endures the beating of small fists, loving us at our worst. And if we remember our tantrums we remember the rage—not only the anger at being thwarted—but the greater rage of being loved all the same, when we would deny our relationship with her and with others. It is the hardest thing in the world for little children to pass through the terrible loneliness of rage to the grief that burns the anger out so that we can accept one another's love. Or God's.

In his ballet *Prodigal Son*, George Balanchine illustrates this interior passage in a way that leaves the observer hollow and exhausted. In the beginning, the son expresses the aggression of youth, his rage and frustration at the love he perceives as confinement. He turns away from home and crouches like an animal ready to spring, pounding his knee with both fists.

When the father tries to include him in the family blessing, he pulls away. The father gently insists, but the moment his back is turned, the son repeats the gesture and explodes into the immense leap that became Villella's and Barishnikov's trademark. The ballet progresses to the son's inevitable downfall and abandonment. He is totally alone. His loneliness is unbearable, even more unbearable than love. It is the pain of acknowledging that he is not a separate entity in the universe that brings him through grief and sets him on his way to his father's arms.

The wrath of God is relentless compassion pursuing us when we are at our worst. Christ give us mercy to bear your Mercy!

There are many of these movements of repentance in solitude— yours and mine—this becoming aware of the security blanket of sins that are as unfathomable as they are unspeakable. We have tantrums each time this childish totem is taken away, and we begin again and again to turn to the unbearable love of God. Always we begin; we are continually beginning. Beginning to understand what loneliness really is: hunger for God.

We try to fill up that ghastly hole in the pit of our stomachs that is really in our souls. We try to fill it with food, with power, with sex. And there is no more isolating loneliness than that experienced in the most intimate act between two people when they are using it to take instead of give.

We begin to realize that this hunger will never be satisfied, not in this life. It is the hunger to see the Face of God, and the only possible food is prayer, prayer that is all of our lives, to yield to God's emptiness, vastness, to lose control of our ideas of God, our ideas and stereotypes of ourselves, of prayer. We finally—again and again—let go all our concepts of God and begin to understand God's notion of us.

At this point in the relationship I always want to turn and run. I feel the same way when I am about to commit myself to a river. At times I do a lot of whitewater canoeing. You use a canoe without a keel to avoid scraping rocks near the water's surface. You have a paddle, your instincts, and maybe some rocks in the bow for ballast. Maybe the rocks in our heads are ballast for the solitary interior journey.

You learn to read the water so that after you have passed through a tranquil stretch and come to rapids, you take what seems the most dangerous path down the dark V of current to the boiling, violent haystacks of white water that are paradoxically the smoothest way to stillness. You try to go into the rapids more slowly than the current so that at least in the beginning you have a little control.

But then as you float down, your heart lurching visibly in your body, you realize you have passed a point of no return: you are committed. There is nothing much you can do except to trust your skill, your reactions, and your boat, to try to avoid rocks and treacherous eddies marked by smoother, more inviting water, and the great holes, the vortices, that can swallow a canoe and destroy it.

The river can kill you.

So can God.

But the difference in solitude is that you begin to learn that even if you do plunge into one of those seemingly bottomless holes, you are still cradled in the hollow of God's hand. You are borne by Love.

However, solitude doesn't always or even frequently include this sort of terror.

Sometimes I feel like a little child happily rummaging in an eschatological toy box: the toys are icons and the play is for keeps. One of the toys in this box is a theological construction set. It isn't safe to hang anything on the models I build with it, but they catch light refracting from the soul.

Sometimes solitude is like balancing on the edge of a razor blade with a meadow full of wildflowers on one side and madness on the other. Or solitude is like a tea ceremony, the celebration of life in all its homely movements taken out of time.

In solitude is the wonder of the commonplace, the mystery of ordinary life: eating, sleeping, reading, listening to God's secrets and jokes, a sense of delight, of dance, of fruition, learning that solitude is not something we need to scramble to fill up, but that it is full and overflowing if we can learn to accept the familiarity of insecurity and let go into Silence.

Solitude is the essence of relatedness; solitude is being poured-out-through. We evolve toward simplicity, we dwell in the Word.

After all, solitude *is* ordinary life, though my ordinary is perhaps not your ordinary. On one of the standardized IQ tests there used to be two definitions for the word "normal." One was "according to a universal standard." The better definition was "true to type." When we are being normal we are being true to our own type, our own ordinary, our own solitude, our own unique vocation, and the silence of solitude teaches us to give one another the spaciousness in which this uniqueness can be explored and nurtured for the sake of community.

Often people ask if it isn't frustrating to have exterior solitude interrupted. This is an artificial idea of solitude. We need to learn to live all of life from the wellspring of interior solitude. Perhaps this is one of the keys to living in the madness, the telescoping demands, the assaults and exhaustion of our culture; to explore interior solitude and learn not only not to be afraid of it but also to live out of its self-discipline, its limitless resources and deep Silence, so that we have something to give to the community of creation instead of merely exploiting and devouring it.

For me, interior solitude is normally expressed by having large amounts of physical solitude, whether in wilderness or city. For others it often means something entirely different. For all of us it means interior solitude expressed in ordinary exterior community, no matter how much or how little physical togetherness we may have. Solitude is not confined to the mystique of religious community. Holiness is transfiguration through and within the ordinary.

Self-discipline in this context is the opposite of self-control. When each of us finds the aspiration, the vision of our own ordinary, which is our vocation, the self-discipline necessary to sustain it becomes self-evident, falling into place almost without our noticing—if we are keeping our gaze on God and not on our selves. This does not mean that it is effortless, but the self-discipline that is the consequence of aspiration helps us break out of psychological traps into spaciousness, healing, and wholeness. The self-discipline of aspiration is the struggle to let go, to open a clenched fist.

On the other hand, the self-control that attaches to mere constraint, the fight to squeeze our selves into something that for us is not ordinary, not our vocation, a false stereotype forced on us by our selves or by others who would control and exploit us—this control is the exercise of domination. It is the narcissism of ego that needs always to inflate itself with its own presumption, destructively screwing down the lid, cutting off minds from bodies, denying the glory of unique creatures.

Thus, if we are living out of the resources of solitude in the community in which we find ourselves, we begin to realize that we love one another not merely from herd instinct, but because each of us has the same love for God, the same hungering. We become aware of others' holiness and potential holiness, holiness they are not and cannot be aware of. We become aware of their holiness because we become aware of their hurts and of our share in those hurts. Like John the Baptist, we become lamps, our light leaping toward one another across the darkness that divides us.

Many people came to believe in Jesus through John. We often think of the events in first-century Palestine as a single moment in linear history. We think of prophets as mediums, foretelling the future in time.

They aren't. And there isn't.

More than twenty-five years ago, John Robinson in *Honest to God* attempted to lay to rest the concept of the three-story universe: hell down there, earth in the middle, and heaven up above. In spite of that book and others, we are still making efforts to lay to rest our mental image of linear time and our addiction to linear thinking in a spatial universe.

Space and time are one. Events may seem to have sequence, but there is illusion here. Think of yourself viewing the history of the earth from another point in space; think of God at the center of a sphere whose surface is time, so that all moments are the same for God.

Neither a moment, nor energy vibrating to appear as a particle, can be grasped: we are engaged in a cosmic dance that continues whether or not we choose to acknowledge it, whether or not we choose the isolation of denial. Solitude is coming to be in the possibility inherent in fluid interrelationship that knows not up or down or linear time, but only the coordinates of grace.

Physicists tell us that "talking about an experience of timeless present is almost impossible because all words like 'timeless,' 'present,' 'past,' 'moment' refer to the conventional notions of time. Events only seem sequential. Our concept of time is a convenience, nothing more."

Interpenetrating our universe in time is God's no-time, which is all time and transcends time. The Christ event is not a breaking *into* history but a breaking *open* of history, to show who God is and how God acts throughout creation from eternity.

We wrestle with the first and second comings, but they are one. It is the God of the burning bush who is born in the straw and does not consume. The apocalypse begins with creation. We say, "*Maranatha*, come quickly," but Christ indwells and transfigures the creation now.

The prophets and apostles knew this spaciousness of sacred time and wrung it from their language in an effort to break us free. Isaiah proclaims, "Thus says the Lord, 'Behold I create new heavens and a new earth; and the former things shall not be remembered or come into mind. But be glad and rejoice forever in that which I create, for behold I create Jerusalem a rejoicing, and her people a joy.'"

And the Letter to the Ephesians: "In Christ God chose us before the world was founded . . . made known to us the hidden purpose—such was God's will and pleasure determined beforehand in Christ—to be put into effect when the time was ripe, namely that the universe, all in heaven and on earth, might be brought into a unity in Christ."

Release from the tyranny of time enables us to break through perspective in our solitude. It is in solitude and silence that we hear and utter the ineffable Name of the One who uttered Being: God is, therefore I AM. The word and the Name are one. And we can neither hear nor speak with words at all, just as Jesus had to use parables to describe the kingdom of God, just as the liturgy of the Eucharist is cosmic shorthand, just as these words are foolishness.

When we hear, when we utter the Word in the silence of adoration, we participate in creation and the healing and transfiguration of creation. We utter Christ as we bear Christ: as our prayer becomes more wordless and imageless, as we participate more deeply in Love, we know the kingdom of God truly within us, that we, like John, are bearers of light, lamps in the windows of God's house, fired with the oil of repentance, burning with Christ as we wait for Christ.

Jesus, Word of the living God, be borne in us today.

There is only one way to approach the questions at the beginning of this essay: you go into the wilderness to be enabled to bear the Word, as the Holy Spirit enabled the prophets to bear it, overshadowed Mary that she might bear him, descended on Jesus, empowering him to reveal, to bare himself as Word made flesh, and at Pentecost bestowed the gifts that empower humanity to bear it too. That is all these gifts are: tools to enable us to bear the Word.

We are all solitaries.

No one can take you into the desert. You must find the path yourself. Plunge into your loneliness, your hunger, your thirst. In the desert you will be purified and tempted; God will speak to your heart and angels will come and minister to you.

Out of the silence of your own solitude, like the prophets you will speak the Word; like Mary Theotokos, the God-bearer, you will bear the Word, and bare Christ to the world.

Almighty and ever-living God,
by your Holy Spirit in the burning bush, in chariots of fire,
and in tongues of flame
you have made your people partakers
in the radiance of your transfigured Christ:
strengthen the hearts of your servants:
give us courage in temptation and comfort in desolation;
show us your paths in the desert
that we may find streams of living water;
make us holocaust for your people,
pure channels of your love,
and receive us into the fire of your life.

www.ingramcontent.com/pod-product-compliance
Lightning Source LLC
Jackson TN
JSHW020021141224
75386JS00025B/643